FUND-RAISING
WITHOUT FAIL

FUND-RAISING WITHOUT FAIL

by

Maureen Spurgeon

PAPERFRONTS
ELLIOT RIGHT WAY BOOKS
KINGSWOOD, SURREY, U.K.

Made and Printed in Great Britain by Robert Hartnoll Ltd, Bodmin, Cornwall.

CONTENTS

For
all my favourite good causes:

The Friends of West Lea School
Friends of Durants School
Eastern Region, The Home Farm Trust
London Region, Association For All Speech Impaired
    Children (A.F.A.S.I.C.)
Westminster Society for Mentally Handicapped Children
    & Adults
Edmonton Branch – The British Red Cross

With heartfelt thanks for all the support, help,
encouragement, companionship and pleasure which they
have given me and my family.

1

WHY FUND-RAISING MUST NEVER FAIL

Once upon a time, fund-raising was a somewhat genteel pastime, mostly favoured by people of leisure – mainly women. Money was usually raised at dainty afternoon teas, by subscriptions and straightforward donations backed up by income from long-established charitable trusts and investments. Education and the care of the sick and needy more or less struggled along at a bare minimum.

Nowadays, of course, fund-raising is a very different matter. With the advance of modern science and technology has come more and more research into all types of disease, illness and disability. Television series and computer learning-aids are widely used in our schools. Senior citizens are living longer, needing extra care and facilities. Thankfully, we are also beginning to have a more enlightened attitude towards handicapped people who are being encouraged to lead more fulfilling and independent lives, very often with the help of specialised equipment and purpose-built premises. Older buildings and services which were originally funded by a local authority require maintenance, refurbishment and modernisation. And it all has to be paid for.

No wonder the number of voluntary fund-raisers always needs to increase!

And no wonder that the public at large frequently seem to adopt rather long-suffering faces at the seemingly endless demands on their pockets.

No doubt about it. Fund-raising is more of a challenge in these modern times than ever before. But getting people to part with their hard-earned cash to help your favourite good cause need not be a wearisome task.

Yes. You *will* be confronted with moans and groans when you start trying to get names for yet more sponsored walks,

7

sponsored swims, sponsored silences. You have probably grumbled about the same thing yourself. And why?

Because there doesn't seem much fun in getting blisters on a sponsored walk. There's no enjoyment or satisfaction in handing over a sum of money when the sponsor form is thrust under your nose. No chance of any prizes. No entertainment value. Nothing much to remember.

But – just think about transforming that well-worn idea of a dreary sponsored walk into an all-comers fancy dress parade through town, or around a convenient park or open space, charging a modest entrance fee for the chance of winning an award or prize . . .

Shopkeepers and restaurant owners are generally very enthusiastic prize-givers once they are invited to judge the competition, particularly if the parade is planned to attract custom outside their premises!

It must result in good publicity for them – and good publicity for your group too. Shoppers and passers-by will also get to know about your good cause in the process, and be ready to put money into collecting buckets and cans as the parade moves along.

Or, why not make that same sponsored walk into a placard parade? (Insult anyone you like for 50p – all in a good cause!) Or, perhaps a Victorian outing with children playing with hoops and tops. Or an old-fashioned 'street party' in the school playground, complete with barrel organ or piano, talent contest and a sing-song?

Family entertainment in which everyone can enjoy taking part is always far more popular than fund-raising attractions aimed at any one specific group, such as the athletes, the swimmers, the young or the comparatively fit.

Doesn't a swimming gala with a programme of displays and novelty events, from the 'apple scramble' (swimming and scrambling for bobbing apples – first team to get ten wins) to the 'balloon push' appear more attractive than an afternoon spent swimming length after length of the nearest pool? Hardly surprising that few people bother to come and watch!

Yet it needs only a little imagination to plan a semi-comedy exhibition of a theme such as 'swimmers through the ages'. A 'duckling disco dance' routine for tinies and non-swimmers at the shallow end, and a display of life-saving and water safety. Definitely worth paying an admission charge to see and enjoy, especially with a fund-raising raffle and refreshments on sale.

And, no – you will *not* sell mountains of dolls' clothes and knitted toys at a bazaar or coffee morning, even if they are on sale at the tiniest fraction of shop prices. The reason is that, of all the visitors to your fund-raising event, only a small percentage are interested in buying knitted toys and dolls' clothes.

Remember, toy shops and babywear specialists are open regularly, six days a week, attracting their own customers from a wide area. Your fund-raiser will only last a few hours.

If you are ever faced with a mountain of left-over knitteds, hold a 'baby sale', or put up an advertisement notice in the nearest ante-natal clinic, hospital maternity unit, or young wives' club. Plenty of interested customers there!

As for dolls' clothes, just buy a cheap, unclothed doll, or dolls, package the clothes into a 'complete wardrobe', and set aside for the next raffle or 'lucky draw' prize.

Then make up your mind to study your market, in the same way as businessmen do, and find out the things which people really *want* to buy. You might start off by making a list of everything you yourself could be buying at the time of your fund-raising event, taking into account any special things such as for summer holidays, birthdays and wedding anniversaries.

You will soon discover that the real reason why a homebake stall is always so popular is because almost everyone needs to buy cakes and biscuits, either as part of their weekly shopping list, or as a family treat. So – why not buy these to help a good cause, and probably save themselves money into the bargain?

Make dozens of milk-jug covers which you would never use in your own home, and the chances are that no would-be customers will fancy them either.

Fun fund-raising is all about making it easier, more of a pleasure than a chore. And the greatest pleasure of all is the sense of achievement that comes from . . . success!

It is all too easy for members of a fund-raising group to set themselves too high a target. In the end, they find that the funds they raise only just keep pace with inflation and their target figure recedes year after year.

So many projects have failed for this very reason. And all because the fund-raisers did not take enough time to sit around a table for an hour or two at the very beginning and work out whether or not it was worth launching an appeal.

On the other hand, it can sometimes be more difficult to spend the money in the way for which it was intended, than actually to raise the funds!

For instance – a short-stay hostel for mentally handicapped youngsters launched an appeal for a swimming pool, and very successful it was too. Only one snag. The committee had been unable to obtain planning permission in writing.

So, when planning permission was refused by the local council, all funds raised were 'frozen' on the grounds that people had been asked to raise the money for the specific purpose of providing a swimming pool. Therefore, the funds could not be spent on anything else.

In the end, by proving that the money was raised with the intention of helping the mentally handicapped youngsters by whatever means, the hostel did manage to get their funds made available to spend on some other much-needed amenity. But this took well over a year, and a lot of wrangling to establish that the fund-raising supporters had not been misled in any way. During this time the frozen funds were not even earning interest in any building society or bank deposit account, and the hostel's general fund-raising efforts were severely hampered.

Proper information and communication would have saved this particularly hard-working group a great deal of disappointment and unnecessary work. And it's unnecessary, unrewarding work which makes fund-raising a failure!

The organisation and planning of your fund-raising events need not be a dull, laborious task either. Believe it or not, there *are* people ready and willing to help your good cause – not only jumble sale and fête-and-bazaar visitors, but also by giving grants and donations, or support in the shape of free gifts, competition prizes, or running fund-raising raffles at office parties or social clubs.

But, they do need to know about you and the exact aims of your fund-raising efforts first.

'In aid of the local school', or 'for the parish church' is not really good enough. Not half so attractive or appealing as 'playground equipment for the nursery class', or 'new chairs for the parish hall'.

People always like to have some positive idea about where their money is going. Even national charities who need to appeal for thousands of pounds each year will help you focus your local-based fund-raising on one particular need, if you ask.

Just one successful event is all it takes to invigorate half-hearted or less-than-energetic support into fresh bursts of fund-raising enthusiasm.

The problem starts if a general air of gloom and disappointment has been allowed to creep in. If an appeal has been too lengthy and there seems no end in sight, then it's time to revitalise your fund-raising, to go back to the beginning and discover where things went wrong. If it cannot be put right, then set aside past failures and start anew on a better footing.

Take the 'fun' out of 'fund-raising' and you're left with nothing. Put the 'fun' back in – and fund-raising becomes something which everyone can understand and take part in, and there's far less danger of failure.

2

OFF TO A GOOD START

Most people are introduced into an existing fund-raising group, rather than needing to start one from scratch. But it's always useful, even for the experienced fund-raiser, to think back and indulge in a mental refresher course, perhaps learning something new alongside the complete beginner.

Besides, it can often be quite astounding to reflect on the bad habits which have been allowed to creep into the most well-established of groups!

To begin with, let us say that you and a few friends have begun to realise a particular need. Before proceeding any further, *do* make quite sure that the solution which you have in mind *could* be put into practice if enough funds were available.

True, no council planning officer would be able to tell you whether or not a building extension could be erected or swimming pool installed without proper specifications and architect's plans. But that same officer could probably advise if there is any particular restriction which would make your idea a definite non-starter.

Assuming all is well, you and your friends get together and decide to appeal for like-minded helpers. You are now ready to plan –

Your inaugural meeting
First of all, you must think up a name for your group, even if this is only to use as a 'working title' for the time being. Just so that people can quickly get to know who you are and what you are doing.

Elect someone from your group to give a few words of welcome to the audience at the start of your inaugural meeting. Nothing more than a pleasant:

"Good evening ladies and gentlemen! My name is Sally Briggs, and on behalf of my friends with me on the platform, I should like to welcome you most warmly to the inaugural

12

meeting of H.E.N.S. – Help Elltingham North School! And I must say how very encouraging it is to see so many people here tonight, for what we all hope will be a very enjoyable get-together, as well as a worthwhile and constructive meeting, which we are sure will be for the good of the school.

As you know, we are at present looking into the possibility of raising enough money to equip a proper computer room for the school, which is why we are all here. And, to give you a little more information, and explain exactly why the school needs this equipment at the present time, I should like to introduce our guest speaker, chairman of school governors, councillor Mrs Joan Aston."

This guest speaker should be someone known to the audience, as well as your group – at least by name – but not a person who is seen within talking distance too often. A vicar or head teacher cannot really be put into the category of 'guest speaker' when they can be approached almost at any time! And audiences do expect to hear a more objective view, together with observations and comments which are unlikely to be exactly the same as ones which they may have heard already.

Choose someone like the chairman of school governors or hospital trustees, local historian, representative from the local health authority or officer of a national charity . . . these charities will *always* put you in touch with guest speakers in or near your area, often equipped with slides, lectures and video films.

Finding a suitable venue very rarely presents any great problem, so the next thing is to set a date. It is always worth taking some extra time and trouble to decide on this, because the date of an inaugural meeting is often adopted as the approximate date for the annual general meeting, when the preceding year's progress may be assessed, with an annual report and presentation of accounts.

Remember too, that each annual general meeting will also provide a good opportunity to interest new members in joining your group, as well as inspiring existing fund-raisers with a new optimism and energy, if only by stating their achievements and getting everyone chatting over past successes and future ideas together.

So do your best to see that the date of your inaugural meeting has some special significance which will set a good pattern to follow in the future. It might be the date when a

church or hospital was founded. The anniversary of a royal
visit. Or more practically, the first return date from half-term
holiday in a new school year!

Whatever the reason, let it give your meeting something
to commemorate, or for people in the community to
remember – and the perfect excuse to invite distinguished
guests and local dignitaries along, with fund-raising coffee-
and-biscuits or cheese-and-wine afterwards.

Then comes the exercise of letting everyone know about
your meeting, either by duplicated letter, posters, announcements on notice boards, or an inclusion in the 'letters page'
section of the local newspapers. Something along these lines
perhaps –

*We should like to invite all members, past and present, of
the Branchline Youth Theatre, along with any parents, friends
and supporters who may be interested, to attend the inaugural
meeting of 'Branchline Audience' next Wednesday, 7th June,
at Millfields Art Centre, Jasper Road, starting at 7.30pm.*

*As readers may remember, Branchline's stage equipment
was damaged by fire at their base at the old Parklands School
last month, and the purpose of this meeting is to see what
support there would be for 'Branchline Audience' in raising
funds to buy new equipment to enable this one-and-only youth
drama group in Millfields to stage some new productions, and,
we hope, become self-supporting.*

*Cllr. Leon Mann, chairman of the Eastgate Drama Festival
Committee, will be our guest speaker, and we are hoping that
as many people as possible will be able to attend, with time
for refreshments afterwards.*

Yours sincerely

Joyce Graham

BRANCHLINE AUDIENCE

You will then find it a great help to draw up an agenda,
which may sound rather formal, until you think of it as nothing
more than a glorified 'shopping list' so that nothing gets forgotten or overlooked. This can be included as part of a duplicated letter. If not, a convenient blackboard and some chalk
will do just as well.

BRANCHLINE AUDIENCE – INAUGURAL MEETING
Agenda

1. Welcome by Mrs Joyce Graham
2. 'Branchline for Youth' – talk by our guest speaker, Cllr. Leon Mann
3. Audience discussion
4. Election of committee
5. Any other business
6. Vote of thanks by Wayne Norris, Branchline's producer
7. Date of first committee meeting

This agenda will also be a useful guide for writing down the 'minutes' or proceedings of the meeting, either in a ring-bound folder or hard-cover notebook, both as the possible basis for a local press item, and as a permanent record – which you will find is needed far more than you might at first imagine.

Look ahead to the future and possible applications for grants and/or financial assistance. Talks to local groups. Letters to newspapers. The prospect of supplying information to the Charities Commission for the purpose of becoming a registered charity. Any one of these will prove to be twice as difficult without being able to refer to your first-ever meeting as a basis for information.

Most important too is a notebook in which everyone present can put their names, addresses and telephone numbers, plus what they are prepared to do.

When it comes to item 3 on your agenda – the audience discussion – this will be chaired by the guest speaker, and it is worth bearing in mind that one or two questions or comments from experienced fund-raisers are sure to spark off discussion among the first-timers.

After all, each one will have read your letter of invitation with sufficient interest to attend the meeting, so they should have some idea about the support which they can offer, plus any suggestions which they may have in mind.

Election of committee officers

These will be your *chairman*, *secretary* and *treasurer*, plus a *vice-chairman* to take meetings in the chairman's absence. Strictly speaking, each officer should be proposed by one person, seconded by another, and a vote taken if there is more than one nomination.

The *chairman* is basically the organiser, the person whose

job it will be to co-ordinate the activities of everyone on the committee, so that – for example – nobody turns up expecting to do a job which someone else has already agreed to do. He also 'chairs' the meetings and keeps order.

The *secretary* does the 'donkey work' – takes down the minutes of each meeting and enters them in the minutes book, so that all committee decisions are recorded, and that jobs allocated are down in writing, in order to avoid dispute or misunderstanding later.

Helping the chairman to draw up each agenda and notifying each member of the committee of forthcoming meetings, correspondence, telephone calls, contact with local newspapers . . . it all falls to the secretary's lot. So, all the better if you can elect an *assistant secretary* to help ease the load, especially at busy times. And there'll be plenty of those!

The *treasurer* often proves to be the most difficult person to attract, mainly because so many people fight shy of having to handle money and add up figures. Yet a housewife can be just as effective a treasurer as a professional accountant or retired bank manager. Often better, in fact, because the professional money-person may tend to look upon the committee job as a work-a-day chore, when what is really needed is a practical, budget-conscious mind and an eye for a bargain – absolutely essential when you go shopping for the best return on a bank deposit or investment account.

Any other business

The part of the agenda which every committee member looks forward to! On this occasion, the audience discussion should have dealt with any general enquiries, so it is a chance for the chairman to introduce the topic of funding the committee for initial expenses such as stationery, telephone calls, postage stamps, etc. and invite suggestions for an annual subscription. £1 per person or couple is reasonable for an initial subscription, though a higher annual figure may be appropriate later. A bank account must be opened in the group's name, after the first committee meeting.

The audience should also be asked to collect fund-raising items, such as trading stamps and cigarette coupons which can be exchanged for cash or competition and raffle prizes, as well as the 'cash refund' offers which appear on so many consumer products nowadays.

Finally, make sure that each person has a contact telephone

number in order to pass on any gifts, ideas or suggestions, before closing the meeting with a convenient date for your –

First committee meeting
Word of honour – this is the very last agenda you will find in this book! The one and only reason it has been laid out for you to follow is that it can set the whole pattern of your fund-raising, and influence whether your project fails or succeeds.

AGENDA

1. Apologies for absence (*to be recorded*)
2. Minutes of inaugural meeting (*these are not signed by the chairman, until they are read out again at the annual general meeting!*)
3. Matters arising (*from the minutes*)
4. Correspondence (*if any*)
5. Chairman's report (*anything of interest happening, or any new developments since inaugural meeting?*)
6. Treasurer's report (*here, the committee must be informed of the current financial position, and whether the treasurer has any particular preference as to where the funds should be banked*)
7. Target and appeal

Your TARGET and APPEAL item is crucial. It could literally make or break your fund-raising efforts – and it is all because of rising prices and inflation, particularly in property matters.

Some years ago, for example, a covered, heated swimming pool was first priced at a modest £18,000. Two and a half years later, when the fund-raising committee were approaching that target, the cost had risen to an estimated £35,000. Another eighteen months – with £25,000 in the bank – and the cost was £52,000. Until, six years after the start, the target had reached an astronomical £92,000 with funds standing at just £33,000.

This sad state of affairs was mainly due to a serious lack of support and co-operation in the early stages which severely hampered the committee's attempt at any kind of public appeal or appeals campaign. This in turn made it almost impossible to foster public awareness from the very beginning – success at which always results in more offers of help and support.

Inspiring and creating this public awareness can be a challenging business, particularly when it may be difficult for the layman to appreciate a special need. See a group of healthy-looking deaf children playing organised games in the park, and it can be hard to imagine why they should need computer equipment for a language laboratory to help them communicate. Similarly, some people cannot understand why preservation groups need funds to rebuild a steam locomotive, when the days of steam railways are long since gone.

But once fund-raising groups do start a campaign of putting their message across, at least part of that message usually gets through in the end.

So, consider your fund-raising target calmly. If the committee have managed to get any specific quotations, plump for an amount nearer the top end of the scale, rather than the very lowest costing. Unfortunately, prices do go up rather than down, so it pays to be realistic.

Then, work out roughly how much you expect to raise in the first year. Not how much you *hope* to raise. But how much you can *reasonably expect*. The local press is a good source of information on how much other groups have raised at events such as bazaars, fêtes, etc., so try to make a comparison with a group similar in size and appeal to yours.

Set up a suggested programme of events along these lines:

Christmas bazaar	£1,000
Summer fête	£1,000
Three jumble sales @ £200	£600
Six fund-raising events – i.e. one very two months, @ £150	£900
Raffles, talks and other events	£500
TOTAL	£4,000

If your target is more than double your expected yearly income, you need to launch an appeal. Otherwise rising costs may continuously wrest your aims further and further from your grasp.

Meanwhile, it is a good idea for the treasurer to examine what banking facilities and investment terms would be available for your good cause.

With more and more fund-raising being done, charity-type funds are fast becoming big business for banks and building societies, and you will find most of them only too happy to meet the treasurer and advise on the most profitable accounts for your needs, and the best way of banking your money.

One particular treasurer I know managed to increase funds

by at least £150 monthly interest on a special investment account into which a modest fixed sum was paid regularly which shows how a bit of research and planning can pay off.

The secretary could write a letter or press release for local newspapers, to inform as many people as possible of your aims and ambitions, and to begin making yourselves known.

Start by acquainting the reader with the *need* for your appeal.

Then outline the *solution*, and how this would benefit the community. Mention a particular aspect to which the reader can easily relate such as "We all have to grow old some day!", "Most of us have experienced the pleasure of owning a much-loved pet", or "Membership of our junior football club is open to any lad in the area".

Next comes the *appeal*, with the name of your group, and the amount you intend raising.

Lastly, any fund-raising plans for the near future. Like this:

Sir
As many of your readers may already know, the Northway Senior Citizens' Club is in urgent need of an extension to provide space for visiting foot clinics, health visitors and advisors, as well as those members wanting to do handicrafts, etc. The disused garages at the back of Northway offer the space needed, and we have been told by the council that a suitable conversion could be carried out, housing a workshop, small library, medical room and canteen, to benefit not only our present senior citizens, but also those in years to come. And we all have to get old some day!

That is why the newly-formed Friends of Northway will soon be launching an appeal for support in reaching our estimated £80,000 target, and we hope that we may count on everyone's support when the time comes.

Meanwhile, we shall be holding a bring-and-buy sale at Northway next Saturday at 2 pm, when we hope to see as many visitors as possible. And whether they 'bring' a Rolls Royce, or 'buy' a paperback book, it all goes to help our senior citizens look forward to a more comfortable and fulfilling life in their years of retirement.

Yours faithfully
Douglas Leslie
Chairman, FRIENDS OF NORTHWAY

At this stage, it is often best for the officers to concentrate their efforts on making arrangements for the public appeal, while other committee members and helpers channel their energies towards fund-raising which can establish a source of regular income. This is sure to impress everyone attending the appeal launch, as well as demonstrating your initiative, enthusiasm and determination to succeed.

TALK THE CIRCUIT

Start off with one or two members going to the local authority offices (where you pay your rent or your rates!) and asking at the reception or information desk for a list of women's fellowships, mother-and-toddler groups, young wives' clubs – in fact, anyone who could be expected to welcome a guest speaker at one of their gatherings, in return for a £10 – £20 donation to your funds. An offer hardly any club could refuse!

A successful speaker does not necessarily have to talk about your appeal either. I often give talks on palmistry, handwriting analysis and old customs and traditions to raise funds, whilst a fellow committee member's chosen subject is 'The Jewish woman in the home' – very entertaining and most informative for non-Jewish groups! Another friend keeps audiences very well entertained with his knowledge of Victorian music hall. Someone else demonstrates cake decorating. Yet another lady brings an album of old photographs and birthday cards as a focal point for her audience.

Of course, some people do make boring speakers, so it is often wisest to give newcomers a 'run through' on an audience composed of group members, or chosen people who are recommended by someone in the group.

Write down all the subjects in which the committee and suitable helpers are interested, or in which they have had experience, and you will soon find that the list is apparently endless. In fact, the one danger might be the mistake of approaching too many groups at once, and running the risk of being 'snowed under' at any one time. A maximum batch of six letters per 'talker' is a reasonable start.

Your group may be lucky enough to be offered a few engagements before the appeal launch. In that case, each speaker can broadcast the message whilst smilingly accepting the cheque, and then inviting a representative to attend.

Once established, the 'talk circuit' is an excellent way of getting your good cause widely known, as well as meeting lots of different types of people and making plenty of new contacts – perhaps raising extra funds with sales of fancy goods, craft items, sweets or cakes afterwards. The perfect way to end a pleasant evening or conversational afternoon!

Ideally, the person who draws up the list of clubs and fellowships should also be appointed *social secretary*, with the job of compiling a rota of would-be talkers and their chosen subjects, keeping an appointments diary, and maintaining liaison between the committee and the women's groups, so that everyone concerned gets to know whom to contact.

SELL A DIARY

Another member could be *diary correspondent* for the sell-a-diary fund-raiser. So simple an idea, you will wonder why you haven't thought of it before.

The main essential, as you might expect, is a diary. Any diary. No matter if it is last year's forgotten Christmas present. Plus either a duplicate book, or second diary. Then 'sell' each date in the diary, say for £1 per date.

You will find that grandmas will want to commemorate grand-children's birthdays in this way; wedding anniversary dates for husbands and wives; driving test successes, house-moving dates, etc., etc., with each 'buyer' writing their name and address or telephone number on the date in the diary, and details copied into the second diary, or duplicate book. The buyer keeps one copy, and the other goes into a 'lucky dip' drum or tub on a particular date – maybe the day of your appeal launch, or whenever all the diary dates are sold.

Then, the first three dates picked out of the drum or tub win a cash prize, deducted from the takings. When you have sold all the dates in one diary for £1 a time, it makes the grand total of £365 or £366 – take away £150 for a £75 first prize; £50 second prize and £25 third prize, leaving at least £215 to go into your funds!

BOTH BORROWER AND LENDER BE!

A *lend-and-loan officer* might be appointed to start up a borrower's club, details of which can be announced as part of the public appeal.

The basic plan is to get as many people as possible to compile a list of around twenty items which they could make available for loan. Almost anything can go on each list – cat baskets; wallpapering tables; camping equipment; typewriters; hedge-cutters, carpet shampooers . . . If everyone tries to remember the things which they have been asked to lend out as a favour at any time, the list almost writes itself.

Then, anyone who wants to belong to the borrower's club gets a copy of all the lists, and agrees to pay a set rate to the fund-raising group, either on a monthly basis, according to how many items are borrowed during a particular time, or a separate payment for hire per item. Even at £1 hire charge per item, it can be quite amazing to see how funds mount up over a relatively short period of time, and your club will be doing everyone a favour into the bargain.

AND ONE FOR THE SENIOR CITIZENS . . .!

Lastly, do not overlook older helpers or members of your fund-raising group, nor anyone who may be housebound. With them particularly in mind, you might like to think about buying a metre or so of white sheeting, and charge people 50p each to sign their names on it, ready to be embroidered afterwards, then displayed and used eventually as a commemorative or ceremonial table-cloth.

The same idea could also work very well with people signing their names on patches which would later be sewn together and made into a patchwork quilt, either for a raffle prize, for use by your own good cause, or as a goodwill gift for the local community to send to a refugee camp or children's centre in Africa. So, step forward the committee's *craft organiser!*

In fact, it is always best to give *every* fund-raiser a definite job to do, whether on a temporary or permanent basis. Members are always far more likely to attend committee meetings regularly and take an added interest in what is going on if they also know that they are making a special contribution of their own, and have a particular purpose in being in the group.

And if all this sounds like hard work – well, fund-raising usually is. But there is *always* twice as much back-tracking and double-checking if everything is haphazard and disorganised to begin with, and nobody terribly sure of what they are supposed to be doing.

That is why fund-raisers always are best working to a well-planned schedule, knowing that everything has been properly organised.

3

LAUNCHING AN APPEAL

Many committees, particularly if they are newly formed or small in size, find the idea of an appeal rather daunting. Hence the fairly common mistake of concentrated fund-raising for two or three years, realising that the target figure is mounting due to inevitable price rises, and *then* launching an appeal, more as an act of desperation than anything else. By this time, of course, people have already experienced lots of fund-raising, and want to see some evidence of their support, rather than an appeal to try and raise more money than anyone had bargained for.

A successful appeal does not have to be an appeal on a lavish scale. But it does have to make people interested in your cause. Really interested. So that they want to know what you will be planning next, when your group hopes to put future schemes into operation, and what it will mean in real terms.

A dinner or presentation to launch your appeal is not too difficult to arrange, provided that you set your sights on a date at least six months in advance.

Mid-spring is a good time, because you will then be able to take advantage of the milder weather to plan a complete programme of fund-raising events over the five or six months following the appeal. Lots of ideas and suggestions in Chapter 8 – *Money Spinners*, and more than enough for your group to have something at least every month.

Once you and your committee have a provisional date in mind, you will need to decide between a set meal laid on by caterers, or a buffet prepared by the fund-raising team, as this will probably influence your choice of venue.

There are advantages to both possibilities. The set meal is usually a high-class presentation, designed to attract the wealthier people, with a top table for guests of honour, etc. It is surprisingly difficult for people to refuse their support once they have been wined and dined!

The whole presentation can be a money-spinning enterprise

itself, adding a profit to the charges for the hire of the venue, cost of the meal, and perhaps, a disco or dance band, to determine the price of the tickets, as outlined in the 'profit margin' paragraph in Chapter 8.

However, should you find that a limited choice of venue or the location of your fund-raising group makes an appeal presentation of this kind rather too complicated to manage, a buffet meal on a smaller scale can work just as effectively. The buffet must not be a continual attraction, and there must be enough seating accommodation for all who attend. The main advantage here is that the event will be cheaper, so more people can afford to attend.

Once you have set a date, booked a venue and decided on a meal, the next task is to draw up a guest of honour list. Members of parliament, local politicians and officials may often be a good choice, not least because much of what they say and do is inevitably recorded in the press and on local radio, and this will help get your fund-raising more widely known.

Almost all mayors preside over a special charitable fund during their year of office. Although this does not rule out the mayor's supporting as many good causes as he or she wishes, it is likely that one or two particular projects will have been especially designated for the mayoral year.

But the deputy mayor is another matter. Being the mayor's second-in-command, he or she is unlikely to be quite so committed to specific fund-raising, which means your group could well have more success in getting support over a longer period.

It is also worth reflecting that a deputy mayor this year could step into the mayor's car the next . . .

It pays to be prompt in contacting your proposed guests of honour, and all the better if one or two committee members can make a personal visit by appointment.

PUT IT INTO PRINT

Then you can get some quotations for printed invitations, remembering to state the price of the tickets, who the guest(s) of honour will be, and whether dress is to be formal or informal. Guests of honour are not usually expected to pay for their tickets, although many do prefer to donate this amount.

100–150 people at an appeal dinner is about average, which will be the number of tickets printed. Many printers offer a price reduction for more than one job, and so, if you are planning a menu, do take this along at the same time, together with a rough lay-out for a souvenir brochure. Sheets of paper folded to represent pages of the required size and a rough cover outline is all the printer will want to see at this stage, in order to give a price which should also specify the cost of a reprint run.

Much of your brochure will be based on the programme of fund-raising events, (one page per event, in date order), preceded by a brief history of the purpose of your appeal. Explain what it will accomplish, print photographs of any relevant details, such as the proposed site, local well-wishers and dignatories taking an active part, etc. interspersed with one or two pass-the-time puzzles centred on some aspect of your appeal. Let there be a couple of prizes to be won, such as free admission tickets to a forthcoming fund-raising event!

The souvenir brochure can have any number of pages, including advertisements and well-wishers' messages for your appeal. All of these will need to be paid for, in order to off-set your printing costs and make a profit! Base your advertising space on half-pages – generally the most popular size with business concerns – priced on the basis of half the cost of the cheapest display advertisement in the local newspapers. Think in terms of getting a group of eight advertisements to make up both sides of a double-page spread.

Estimate for the minimum quantity which your printer will accept – usually at least 350, to make it an economical proposition. And if members of the committee do as much of the layout and art-work as they can between them, this will keep printing charges to a minimum. Later on, you will also be able to photocopy those pages which apply to particular fund-raising events at the appropriate time, to use as publicity material, with the souvenir brochure offered for sale throughout the whole of the six-month period.

Next step is to compile a list of possible guests. Anyone who you think will be interested in supporting your project.

For instance, are you appealing for funds in respect of a community project, such as a school, college, church, special medical or social unit, or hospital? Then list the names of all pupils, parents, patients, members, parishioners or staff, both past and present, making particular note of any who you know are currently employed or involved in any kind of business venture, plus a list of any former members of previous fund-raising committees.

Continue with the names of local businesses, especially those who supply or who may be in the immediate neighbourhood of the focus of the appeal.

Committee members and supporters should also approach the managers of their banks and building societies, as many have special allowances for donations to local fund-raising activities. However, many banks will ask if the fund-raising group's bankers have already made a donation, so do not neglect to approach them first.

Draft an appeal letter, something along these lines, to be sent off about four months before the date of the appeal launch.

Dear . . .

The Friends of Northway are organising a special appeal to raise funds for an extension to the old people's club at Hightown. And, as a member of the committee, I am hoping that we may have the pleasure of inviting you and a partner to a special appeal dinner on 12th April at the Rockpool Hotel, Hightown, at 7.15 for 8.00 pm. Tickets are just £... each, and the guest of honour will be the Rt Hon Earl Raymond, MP.

The appeal will continue until (date of last fund-raising event) with a special programme of fund-raising events throughout the spring and summer. Details of all these will be contained in a special souvenir brochure with advertising space for businesses at the rate of £... per half page.

We shall also very much welcome donations, both large and small, towards appeal funds. Alternatively, you may like to help by organising a fund-raising event or raffle within your firm or social club. If necessary, we shall be pleased to provide tickets and prizes so that you are not involved in any out-of-pocket expenses.

All we want is to give our senior citizens the help and facilities which they so badly need, and we know you will do all you can to help us. Please use the reply slip provided, if you find this convenient.

Yours sincerely

....

FOR THE FRIENDS OF NORTHWAY COMMITTEE

REPLY SLIP

I enclose * .... to pay for .... tickets for the appeal
dinner
                    * .... as a donation towards the appeal
I would be interested in
*taking an advertisement in the souvenir brochure
*organising a raffle or fund-raising activity
*Delete as necessary
Signature .... Telephone number ....

Try to have your souvenir brochure and tickets ready at
least one month before the date of the appeal dinner, so that
you can send brochures to all local newspapers, backed up
by a news item and later, an invitation for them to report on
the occasion.

Most important of all, do make sure that all guests at the
appeal dinner are aware of your forthcoming fund-raising
activities. And, to get off to an impressive start, ask one of
your guests of honour to mention the choice of a covenant
deed, or membership of a 'one hundred club' for all those
present, as well as their friends, relatives and business colleagues.

To form a *one hundred club*, you need one hundred people
each contributing a small monthly amount. In the UK this
could be £12 per year, either paid annually, £6 half yearly or
£3 quarterly, and paid by banker's order. Then every month
there is a draw which can always coincide with a fund-raising
event to bring more people's attention to the advantages of
supporting your group, with the attraction of winning one of
three cash prizes – i.e. £20, £10 and £5 or whatever value of
cash prizes is deemed to be suitable by the fund-raising committee. Every three months the £20 first prize might be
increased to £50; and at the end of the year, the club may
like to offer an extra bonus cash prize – say, £20 – open to
all non-winners throughout the year. Around half the projected £1,200 income should be given back in prize money.

In the same way you could form a *two hundred club*, or
your one hundred club could be based on a £2 per month
subscription in prosperous places. Either change would
double the profits and the prizes too of course.

So make sure that all committee members have plenty of
note-books for names and addresses, and the treasurer is
equipped with a supply of standing order forms to sign!

A *deed of covenant* offers even more benefits to your fund-raising group. This takes the form of a yearly donation, with the actual amount being decided by the supporter. This amount, the supporter pledges over a minimum period of four years for a registered charity, and seven years for a non-charitable cause. The ruling factor is that your fund-raising cause must be capable of going on for more than the covenant period, and this is almost always the case.

COVENANT FORM

I (name ....) (Mr/Mrs/Miss/Title ....)
of (address ....)
undertake that, for four years (or my lifetime, whichever is the shorter) I will pay to (name of cause ....)
a sum which, after deduction of income tax at the basic rate, will leave £ ...... (actual amount to be given) starting on the (date ....).
Signed ....
Signature of witness ....
Address of witness ....
..

The key phrase is – 'after deduction of income tax at the basic rate' – because this means that your fund-raising cause receives not only the actual donation, but can also claim from the Inland Revenue the sum of income tax deemed payable on that amount. i.e. if a person paid £5 per year, the fund-raising cause would actually be richer by £6.85 to include £1.85 tax deemed payable (if basic rate tax were 27%).

This covenant scheme applies to all parts of the United Kingdom. But there are many other tax schemes and allowances which can benefit charities and good causes throughout the world, so there is no telling how much your funds may be boosted for the sake of a few telephone enquiries, and perhaps a little detective work.

For further information about covenants, see Appendix (1), page 121.

Lastly, the secretary must make a note to write letters to all local papers after the appeal, saying how much money has been raised, what the prospects are, and inviting people to organise fund-raising activities or raffles.

4

WHO WILL GIVE YOU MONEY?

Charitable trusts exist to help good causes which the trustees consider to be worthy of financial assistance.

But, mention charitable trusts in the company of seasoned fund-raisers, and the response is likely to be a mixture of slow-spreading smiles and long-suffering sighs – depending of course, on whether funds have been boosted by sizeable donations or not.

Yet, theoretically at least, one project should stand just as good a chance as any other when it comes to getting money. So, what goes wrong? Why should one fund-raising group be favoured more than another?

The answer lies within the constitution of each trust, how that trust is to be administered, and the purposes for which it was established. It is no use approaching a trust set up for relieving the plight of abandoned dogs if your group is seeking help for the church restoration fund.

Some charitable trusts, particularly in the UK, date from those bygone times when good souls would set aside money to provide woollen stockings for thirty honest spinsters of the parish, or drinking fountains for workhouse children – and there are many such minor charitable trusts whose purpose has now become defunct. But, legal arguments remain as to whether the funds of such a trust can be administered for any other purpose, or indeed, if the trust can be wound up.

This is why trust funds founded in later years list their objectives as 'general charitable causes', to avoid such difficulties in the future. It does not mean they are willing to give donations to any group who cares to ask.

Pay a visit to your local reference library, and you will find well over two thousand charitable trusts and trust funds listed within the pages of 'The Directory of Grant-Making Trusts' (see Appendix (2), page 121).

LOCAL CAUSES – LOCAL FUNDS

If you are seeking a grant or donation on behalf of a local cause, then apply to local sources first..Call at your reference library, and ask to see any details or information available on trusts *apart* from those listed in the main directory – and you should find that these are local ones.

Alternatively, the local historian or information officer could help since at least one of the trustees or perhaps the secretary to the trustees is likely to be a person who either lives or works in the area.

Once you have the name of a trust, it is usually easy to trace the name and address of the person to whom applications should be sent, plus a brief outline of the history of the trust, its aims, and the type of project it is designed to help. For further assistance, see Appendix (3) (page 121).

Even if you are informed that all funds are exhausted, it is never a waste of time making your group and its aims known. One day there might be another chance and anyway the trustees of one trust fund are often trustees of another, and so may be able to refer you to another source of help. And the same rule applies to local voluntary organisations who assist in fund-raising.

All charitable trusts will need to be satisfied that you are at least in the process of a concentrated local appeal for funds at the time of applying. Proof of this appeal can be provided in the form of copies of appeal letters sent to local businesses, together with a proposed mailing list, and names of businesses who have made donations, along with the amount in each case. Some charitable trusts are restricted to a limited geographical area in which they are able to offer financial assistance, usually awarding other grants only to projects of potential national interest.

MAKE YOUR PURPOSE CLEAR

Charitable trusts do *not* usually contribute to a general fund.

Your application needs to be for a specific purpose – and, if this is aimed at local level, you must show that:

a) your proposed project would have lasting benefit, not only in the immediate area, but beyond;

b) that your project is seeking to provide a facility which fulfils a very real need to part or whole of the community;
c) that the facility for which your fund-raising group is aiming would be unlikely to be provided through any other source; and
d) that there is a pressing need for your aims to be realised as soon as possible.

HOW MUCH MONEY?

You cannot afford to be vague about this. Clearly state your proposed target, how much money has been raised so far, and what has been achieved, your projected income over the next twelve months, and how much money you expect to raise from other sources.

If you are asking for a contribution to make up the balance of a proposed target, then you must give precise details as to how you plan to go about raising the rest of the money needed.

Equally important is how your group intends to spend the money! No use making an appeal for a building based on various estimates received without taking into account the furniture, soft furnishings, fittings and equipment needed before anyone can benefit.

Similarly, it is clearly unwise to make an appeal for a much-needed minibus if your group cannot state precisely how that minibus will be funded or eventually replaced. Any trust could rightly argue that once a particular facility has been provided, it is always doubly hard to manage once it is no longer available.

CAN YOUR PROJECT SUCCEED?

This is the most important factor of any application for financial assistance.

Your committee must prove by evidence of support, progress in fund-raising, locally-based appeals, firm promises of financial assistance (e.g. deeds of covenant) etc. that there is sufficient interest in the project to make it a worthwhile proposition. It really is a waste of time writing to charitable trusts on a 'wishful thinking' basis – wanting something for the best possible reasons, but having no clear idea or really positive plans as to how the target is to be achieved. Probabilities, hopes of lucky chances and untried possibilities are simply not a good enough basis.

And, if you do receive money for a specific project which subsequently fails, then all such monies must be offered back to the various benefactors – which, in turn, might affect any further appeals in the future.

HOW LONG WILL YOU NEED FINANCIAL SUPPORT?

In other words, is your group seeking a single grant or donation towards a particular project, such as a building restoration programme, or special facility for which upkeep and maintenance have already been agreed? Or is it proposed merely to form the nucleus of a scheme which in time may be extended and improved upon, and which will therefore need funding over a period of years?

CAN YOU DUPLICATE LETTERS TO TRUSTS?

The answer to this question is always an emphatic *no*! Each letter to each trust you approach must be written separately, and with particular reference to the aims of that trust.

For instance – let us suppose that your group is fund-raising for a play and leisure area for handicapped children and their families. Such a project would cover aspects of welfare, plus health, environmental and social benefit for years to come.

So, if a trust were specifically aimed at welfare, then it is the welfare of those children and their families which you need to concentrate on, by showing that the proposed play area would be providing a place where families could meet in safety and privacy, for children to play and parents to enjoy a break from the demands of looking after a handicapped child.

Such a project might also appeal to a trust whose objectives are primarily concerned with education, because those children attending the play area could learn skills there which they would find almost impossible to acquire elsewhere – such as kerb drill, and riding a bicycle unaided.

A play area of this nature could also be looked upon as a pioneering scheme, which groups in other areas could learn from and copy, to the benefit and advantage of many more children and their families than those envisaged in the original appeal. And trusts are often impressed by original ideas being put into practice and breaking new ground.

By all means mention and refer to the main benefits offered by your project. But do not lose sight of the aims and constitution of the trust to whom you are applying.

IS IT WORTH SENDING A PRELIMINARY LETTER?

For larger charitable trusts and trust funds at national level, the answer is YES – just as long as you make it clear that it *is* a preliminary letter, and not an actual application upon which a grant may be awarded or reluctantly refused.

MONEY FROM BUSINESSES

Many a charitable trust or trust fund has been founded or is administered by a large company with a factory, store or branch office in or near the area which would benefit from your proposed project.

If this is the case, then write to ask if your group could be 'adopted' as a favourite good cause to benefit from raffles and fund-raising schemes based at sports and social clubs, as well as requesting a donation from the trust fund itself.

Such an approach would also be to your group's advantage at Christmas-time, when many business concerns set aside an amount to donate to fund-raising causes – and most companies give preference to applications from those known to them, or members of their staff.

TV AND RADIO APPEALS

This type of 'mass media' appeal has become very popular in recent years, particularly when raising money for projects involving children and old people.

In common with charitable trusts, no television or radio appeal will consider contributing to a general fund. Nor will they allow any donation, even if designated for a particular purpose, to be put into a general fund until such time as the group is able to spend it. You could not expect money to cover the cost of towels and safety equipment for a swimming pool which has yet to be designed and built. The trustees of this type of appeal always need some tangible proof as to how any proposed donation is to be used.

They also usually prefer to give money to a registered charity. So, if your group is not a registered charity, it makes sense to find one which would be willing to accept any donation on your behalf, should your application be successful.

Local fund-raisers are more likely to receive donations from television and radio appeals transmitted in their own area, such as the popular 'Help a London Child' Easter appeal run by London's Capital Radio. However, many appeals exclude applications for purposes which they feel are adequately funded from other sources.

So, as soon as any media appeal is announced, telephone the television or radio station and ask whether your fund-raising project would be considered. A short but polite rejection is far better than a disappointing refusal in response to a painstaking and time-consuming application which never stood a chance anyway!

5

SPREAD THE WORD AROUND

More fund-raising events end in disappointment through lack of advertising and publicity than for any other reason.

Yet it's often the very last thing on a fund-raiser's mind. It's usually dealt with at the last minute as an after-thought, and not priced properly either. You should set aside an advertising/publicity budget which is roughly the same as the total hire charge for your venue.

NEWSPAPERS

Do you know the advertising rates for your local newspapers? Some fund-raising groups don't bother to find out, and instead persist in setting aside fixed amounts year after year, neither checking how much advertising space their money is buying, nor how many potential customers their advertisement is likely to reach.

So, at least one month before your event, write or call into the local newspaper offices and ask for a copy of their advertising rate card. Most newspapers will also let potential advertisers have a free back number, and you can check whether or not there is any free publicity space on offer – usually in the 'diary of local events' pages. Many newspapers arrange special rates for fund-raising groups as well.

YOUR PUBLIC LIBRARY

Your public library will be able to give you details of any programme of community events, which might offer a free hand-out newsletter service or a monthly 'What's On' information leaflet, featuring local events.

Check the latest deadline date for any free insertions – usually at least six weeks prior to the month of publication.

POSTERS

Start work on these at least six weeks before the date of your fund-raising event, so that you can plan the best possible sites in shops, supermarkets and social clubs where they can be put on display.

Quickest and easiest method is to have one 'master' poster which can be duplicated on a photocopy machine, ready to be coloured in by willing hands.

Just two tips to bear in mind. Firstly, posters in private houses do not generally yield very good results, simply because they cannot normally be seen by passers-by walking along the pavement. And even when they are noticeable, most people do not like to appear to be lingering outside another person's home, for whatever reason.

Secondly, if you want your poster advertised in a public library or building administered by any official organisation or local authority, it is wise to allow a generous measure of extra notice – say, three to four weeks ahead of other posters – because display material often has to be vetted and permission obtained from higher up.

Save your master copy to use for the same event next time. Generally speaking, only the date, and sometimes the admission price has to be altered, with different colours used to ring the changes. Not only will this save your group time and money, but people will begin to recognise your posters after a while, and look forward to events on a regular basis.

LOCAL RADIO
I have always been pleasantly surprised by the willing support given to my favourite fund-raising causes by local radio stations, particularly when it has been possible to turn it into a news story.

See 'additional news items' (page 38) for a few ideas to tempt your local stations, and send out the information about ten days before your event, with a follow-up telephone number.

CAR STICKERS
These have to be *very* bold and lettered in bright colours to have any effect. Yellow does not stand out well as lettering but is a good background colour.

Have at least a couple of dozen extra for identification of helpers on house-to-house collecting for jumble, or offering programmes for sale.

And a balloon-festooned, brightly decorated car always attracts potential customers right up to the day of the event.

BANNERS
Very necessary these, especially on the day itself, even for the humblest of jumble sales. Dregs of ordinary household paint apply readily to a strip of old sheeting or well-worn tablecloth, and the more colours the better.

Confine the date to something like: 'SATURDAY, 2 pm' then your banners can be used year after year.

LEAFLET SLIPS
Very useful as back-up publicity two or three days before the event, particularly for fêtes and bazaars.

Quickest way is to type five or six slips on one sheet of paper which can be photocopied then cut into slips ready to be slipped through doors near the venue, or handed to shoppers on the day. Think in terms of a minimum of 250 slips for letter-boxes, with at least another 500 if you want to tackle the shoppers – double or triple that amount for a densely populated area.

SANDWICH-BOARD MEN
Get an old carton and letter it with details of the fund-raising event, and thread it on to stout string. These are greeted with surprising enthusiasm by would-be sandwich-board men, usually in the shape of children and teenagers, to woo crowds of shoppers.

Most important – send your sandwich-board men out in pairs or groups, and always, for safety's sake, with a responsible, older child or adult in view.

LOCAL SIGNPOSTS
These are essential on the day of your fund-raising event, particularly if the venue is not easily visible from the nearest road or roads. Have them strung up or taped along the route.

Brightly coloured household paint which will withstand the odd shower is ideal for this job. Garages and motor dealers sometimes have cardboard arrows and pointers on give-away advertising material, if you ask. Anything to make your task easier, and the final result more effective.

ADDITIONAL NEWS ITEMS

It's a very dull fund-raising event if there's nothing at all to report! And you will find that the local press are *always* keen to include a news item if it's informative and catches the imagination of their readers.

For instance. Some 'unidentified object' sent in to swell the funds for a jumble sale or flea market. (There's almost always at least one!) Send a quick snap or Polaroid shot into the newspaper office or offices with the news item, and a telephone number which the editorial staff can ring for any more information or comment.

Or write a small feature – about 250 words – on what the fund-raisers are hoping the money will buy. This is always a good news item for the local press. Or maybe the announcement of any special visitors or 'surprise guests' . . .

Send your information into the newspaper offices (typed out double-spaced) or telephone the news desk about ten days before your event. And invite a reporter and/or photographer to come along, if possible.

COMPETITIONS

It is worth taking a little time and trouble to organise a competition to publicise your event. This could be a beauty competition or local talent competition to find a 'queen of the May' or aspiring star celebrity to open your fête or bazaar with modest cash prizes for 1st, 2nd and 3rd. The prize money for the competition need only total perhaps a little over half what you would have spent on newspaper advertising otherwise.

Or you could set aside some of the best gifts for a newspaper competition. This is very popular with editors, particularly if they can inform their readers that it will help a local fund-raising cause!

Include some information about your forthcoming event, and the general aims of your group, with prizes offered, say, for the competitor who can concoct the most words from the name of your fund-raising group. Or, mix up a message into anagram code for competitors to unscramble. Thus:

'PLEASE COME TO THE BOWOOD HOSPITAL

FÊTE' becomes

'LEAPES MOCE OT HET WOBODO SHOPLAIT FEÊT'

Like the idea? Then sort out which type of competition you and your committee would like to try, and start making contacts at least six weeks before the event – especially important for local newspapers who need to have reasonable notice in order to allocate the space.

If you do it properly you will get far more coverage than with an advertisement, and for only half the cost . . .

BLOW YOUR OWN TRUMPET

Publicise your cause at all your events. Give all your guests and visitors information about your aims and what your group is trying to do.

A brief, single sheet is adequate, including a tear-off slip for people to sign with their name, address and telephone number if they would like to join or help your group – or if they wish to be kept informed of future fund-raising activities.

AFTER THE EVENT

Remember to write to the local newspapers, saying how much money you have raised and acknowledging all the help and support you were given and which contributed to the success of the occasion.

Remember too, to mention your next event, and invite both guests and would-be helpers along to swell the ranks!

6

JUMBLE SALES – OR WHITE ELEPHANTS?

A jumble sale is a great way of raising money. It's the easiest event to organise, and there never seems to be any shortage of jumble, nor of customers wanting to come along and spot a bargain.

But jumble sales involve a lot of hard work – and, on occasion, a dispiritingly low amount at the end of the day. Was it worth all the effort?

LOOK AGAIN AT WHAT YOU ARE DOING!
The most common fault with jumble sales is that everything is done in such a rush Putting 'any jumble?' leaflets through letter boxes on Tuesday or Wednesday evenings, ready for jumble collection on Friday evening and the jumble sale on Saturday.

The result? Very often, piles of 'women's and children's' on one table, 'men's clothing' on another. Unwieldy mounds of books and shoes (invariably odd!) scattered on the floor, and larger 'unclassified' items crowded together on the stage under the heading 'bric-a-brac' – or, as a dear friend of mine terms it, somewhat unkindly, 'junk-in-general'.

Like any other fund-raising event, the idea is to make *money* on a jumble sale. At least five times your total expenses, to make it a worthwhile exercise for everyone concerned.

So, if your jumble sales tend to fall below target, what about a fresh image to put some new life into your efforts?

Think about having a new name to begin with. Something like – 'White Elephant Sale'; 'Rummage-Go-Round'; 'Attic Antics'; or 'Bargain Basement' – anything which sounds just a little different and rather more interesting than the well-worn 'Jumble Sale', and makes people curious enough to pause and take more notice when they see your group's activities on the 'forthcoming events' list.

Organise a suitable 'dumping ground' for the jumble, so

that your team can sort everything out without getting in a panic.

Compile a list of people with sheds, garages, spare bedrooms or other would-be storage space, and make plans to begin collecting in good time. Usually this means distributing collection slips asking for jumble, which will need to go out approximately eight days before the jumble sale Saturday.

A supply of two thousand collection slips can either be printed cheaply, or duplicated in the same way as leaflet slips (see page 37). For a twelve-street radius around the venue in a built-up area, this is a reasonable amount for fairly leisurely distribution over a weekend by a group of six helpers.

Give a date when you and your team will be calling to collect jumble. Make it clear which sort of jumble you *don't* want, to save yourself from being lumbered with a moth-eaten mattress, Victorian mangle or anything else which the dustman refuses to cart away. 'No furniture or large items please' is an ideal standby line.

BRANCHLINE YOUTH THEATRE GROUP
BRANCHLINE will be holding a jumble sale to raise funds for some new stage equipment on SATURDAY 29th FEBRUARY at St George's Church Hall, High Street, Wigton, starting at 1 pm. Donations of any suitable items would be most gratefully received, and our collectors will be calling on .... (collectors fill in the appropriate day or evening here) between .... and .... Or you can 'phone Wigton 232881 for a special collection at a time to suit yourself. Many thanks for your help and support.

(P.S. No bedding, or furniture, please!)

A 'return' of 5% on the number of collection slips is about average – so if your group gets more than 100 donations of jumble out of those 2,000 collection slips, they will be doing well.

An alternative method is putting a classified advertisement in the local paper. After all, a 1% return on a modest 10,000 circulation should equal 100 donations, and, taking into account that the cost of an advertisement is likely to be only fractionally more than the cost of printing or photocopying collection slips, many fund-raisers are now opting for this method, with a telephone number in the advertisement for anyone who wants to respond.

However, if you are not too sure about the response you

might get solely from a newspaper advertisement, you could always try the two systems together and see which one yields the best results.

Also remember families, friends and business acquaintances of everyone in your fund-raising circle.

Then, before you set about collecting jumble, borrow a dress rail from a shop or dry-cleaner's, or perhaps one or two tailor's dummies for display purposes. Charity shops are also very obliging, in exchange for a small donation for expenses, or you could ask an amateur theatrical group, school or church committee if they have any equipment which you could borrow for a short time. The success of any jumble sale depends so much on the way in which the goods are presented.

Set aside at least three evenings for collection, and sort out the jumble as you go along. Be quite ruthless about throwing away all extra-grubby items which nobody would buy – it only takes half an hour of jumble sale collecting to recognise these.

Stained and holey clothes should not be displayed but put on one side for disposal to a dealer at the end. The same applies to moth-eaten hats, downtrodden shoes and grimy handbags which should go straight into the rubbish bins, rather than over-crowding precious table space and putting people off buying the better stock.

Bundle up all those out-of-date magazines which you will undoubtedly be given and set them aside ready to sell to the waste paper merchants (information on this source of fund-raising on page 50). Be extra fussy about all accessories, especially hats – never a popular jumble sale item at the best of times.

Sort out all the 'good as new' clothing ready to hang up on a dress rail, if you have one, or makeshift washing line. Luckily, there's never any shortage of wire coat-hangers. And it is really surprising how attractive children's clothing can look pegged out wash-day style both on lines and around the children's stall itself.

Another of my fund-raising colleagues keeps at least two baby dolls to be dressed in clothes for sale in her 'toddlers' togs' corner, with a somewhat aged teddy bear looking very appealing in a T-shirt or football gear, – or, sometimes with a saucepan or casserole dish on his head to promote a few jokey remarks on the household goods counter!

On the actual day of your jumble sale, make sure that all helpers are at the venue at least two hours before 'opening

Fig. 1. A home-made clothes rail.

time', or have a morning sort-out period. Although items will be ready-sorted, there will be tables to be set up, and refreshments to be prepared – always most important for jumble sale fans.

It's a good idea to drape your stalls and counter. This will make your jumble sale less cluttered and untidy, and add a splash of colour from an assortment of borrowed curtains.

Take each curtain by the length, not the width, and pin or tape along the edge of your table on the *wrong* side, with the curtain held upwards, not down, as show in fig. 2. Pleat the fabric as you go along. When you allow the curtain to fall, all pins and joins will be hidden from view, and you will have an attractive, flouncy drape.

DON'T overload your stall, trying to get everything into one enormous pile. With so much buried in an untidy heap, customers will pull and tug in the vain hope of finding something they want, and you will end up actually selling *less*.

Once you have decided which things you want to display, put a reasonable amount of goods on the stall so that customers can see easily what is for sale, and top up stocks at regular intervals – say, every fifteen or twenty minutes – so that people can see fresh items being added. This enables you to maintain interest in your jumble sale all day, or all afternoon, not just for the first half hour or so.

Have one or two helpers on hand with tape measures, and who can also conduct potential customers to a changing area, even if this is only a cloakroom or screened-off corner of the hall, with one or two mirrors within reach.

Good lighting, background music from a radio or tape recorder, groups of chairs set around where customers can

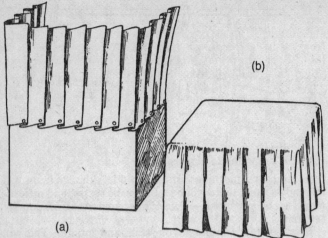

(b)

(a)

Fig. 2. How to drape a stall.
(a) Pin curtain fabric lengthways across top edge on the wrong side.
(b) No joins or pins are to be seen when fabric falls down into place, covering stall.

pause to sort out their purchases and have a chat . . . None of these finishing touches takes more than a few minutes to provide, yet they will all help to make your jumble sale blossom into a more profitable and enjoyable occasion. Jumble sales have a forlorn habit of seeming dull, dingy and rather uninspiring, when there is really no need.

It is also worth planning a few surprises, if you can. Perhaps a 'Worzel Gummidge' lookalike helping to collect door money. A 'going for a song' stall where everything is sold for a specifically small amount. Or a remnant counter – a haven for unpicked zips, buttons and trimmings, which often sell far better in their original, detached state than the garment they were taken from.

You will also find that an 'odds-and-ends' corner is worth particular attention. I remember a part-time antiques dealer who gleefully informed me that she had 'picked up' a Spode dish, marred only by a hairline crack, which led the jumble sale stallholder to suppose that it was worth no more than £1. It was re-sold that same evening for £30.

A local Brownie pack were so pleased to sell my youngest son a die-cast model bus for 2p, due to its battered appearance and complete absence of tyres. With the addition of four tyres from an unwanted toy car, a friend's husband offered £6 to become the new proud owner, only to be outbid by a further £12 from a local collector and dealer the very next day. No wonder my clever son's heart was firmly on that forlorn-looking bus, which is still in his possession!

And my family still recall my good fortune in buying a very mouldy spoon and fork in an equally mouldy-looking presentation case for 10p, which I later sold to my solicitor for £20. When I paid the original 10p, all I wanted was a sturdy case for my collection of knitting needles!

It never takes very long to inspect all china, glasses, paintings and ornaments which you are given. If you have an antiques expert among your fund-raising friends and supporters, consider yourself lucky, and put him or her to work. Otherwise, put aside anything which you think looks a bit better than average, or which you consider just might be valuable, ready to take into a local shop, valuer, dealer or auction room. Chances are they'll buy it for a far higher price than you would have been able to charge at your jumble sale anyway, even if it does not turn out to be a genuine antique or collector's item.

More practical items, particularly glass or crockery, always benefit from a dip in the washing-up bowl. More than once, my friends and I have unearthed complete tea-sets, cheese dishes and soup bowls which proved splendid enough for very popular tombola prizes. In any case, who would actually want to *buy* anything smothered with daubs and smears of dirt and grime?

PRICING

Having weeded out all the rubbishy items, agree on a minimum selling price for each stall. Jumble sale prices always tend to be too low, especially for popular lines, such as household goods and children's clothes, so charge more than you might think at first. In the unlikely event of your price being rejected you can always demote unsold items to a bargain-priced counter after about an hour or so, when any customer is welcome to scramble for a cut-price bargain.

And, what to do with all the stuff that is left over at the end? Pass it on to some other deserving cause!

Thanks to the ingenuity of a member of a local carnival committee, jumble is frequently passed from a fellowship fund for handicapped children, to a youth club, and thence to an old people's group. These days, there are so many fund-raising groups that it is never difficult to track down one or two who are willing to pool resources. You will discover that an exchange of jumble often leads to an extra source of spare helpers, hire of tables, and a whole host of other time-saving, energy-saving benefits which come about through fund-raisers being ready to help each other.

Otherwise, there are the ever-available local dealers who arrange jumble sale collections as a very profitable business sideline. Find them through newspaper advertisements, or by going along to another jumble sale and asking who is operating this service.

Be warned though. Some dealers won't take everything, or only deal in natural fabrics such as cotton or wool, a point well worth clarifying when you make your initial enquiry.

Or – maybe you still have enough energy to gather up the left-overs and head straight into another fund-raising occasion?

Here are a few ideas to set you thinking!

BOOK MARKETS

These are very popular. Who can resist a quick thumb-through or leisurely browse? And think of the students, play group leaders, teachers and others who need all kinds of books for reference purposes!

All this means that you need to collect a LOT of books – the more the merrier. Luckily, people are only too pleased to off-load their unwanted reading matter, and you can always boost your stocks with appeals through features, news items and letters to newspapers, social clubs, libraries and businesses.

You will need to start collecting your stocks much earlier than for a jumble sale – at least a month before the date set for your book market, so that you can sort them out into categories. Something like:

Nursery age books	History
Children's fiction & reference	Non fiction
Novels	Music
Romance	Reference
Science fiction	Commerce

with headings lettered on to cardboard cut from supermarket cartons, or painted banner-like on to strips of sheeting, which will last longer if you intend having more than one book market.

Another tip – keep plenty of boxes and carrier bags handy for your customers, and keep all your pricings based on multiples of 10p to make adding-up easier, and avoid awkward amounts of change.

Many book markets arrange payment on a supermarket plan, with stalls set out in a circular pattern, entrance at one end and 'check out' or payment counter at the other. Purchasers seem to buy more this way, so be sure to have a good supply of helpers taking the money.

Just one last thought – at the first book market I ever helped with, everyone was quite astounded to see a long queue snaking its way back along the road, long before the doors opened. Now it is something to be expected, and the regret is that one cannot manage to organise these ever-popular events more often.

FLEA MARKETS

Flea markets are a very good way of selling off the better stuff among your jumble sale collection, particularly pottery, glass, toys, craft items and the 'dressy' style of clothing, especially fashions from the first half of this century which have become so popular and so collectable during recent years.

Most fund-raising groups manage only one or two stalls, and hire the rest of the floor space to bric-a-brac dealers and small traders. Divide the total hire cost of your flea market premises by (say) ten, then hire out ten stalls at that price, and your group pays nothing for overheads. And you get all the takings from your stall or stalls, plus refreshments and door money!

Use your jumble sale and other fund-raising events to advertise for stall-holders. Bric-a-brac and antique traders are frequent visitors to jumble sales, so pin a notice to a folding table with a sheet for potential customers to sign with their names, addresses and telephone numbers, plus brief descriptions of the goods they intend to sell.

Also draw up a plan of the hall showing the spaces available so that anyone who is interested can mark up the pitch they want to book. This will save any arguments on the big day.

Do be careful that your flea market does not become a glorified jumble sale. Keep secondhand goods strictly to the realms of bric-a-brac in its truest sense, books, records and fashion clothes, making sure that everything is displayed in market stall fashion.

CAR BOOT SALE
This is a favourite because the whole event is so easy to manage and to organise. No tables to get out, no stalls to set up . . . just find a playground or car park and people hand over 'site money' to boost your funds, and that's all there is to it . . .

The secret is to try and make it a fairly regular event so that people get used to the venue. At one place near my home, there is a car boot sale every month, with six fund-raising groups taking it in turns to hire the site and organise a sale twice a year.

This means that the 'car booters' have all become regular customers with these fund-raising groups, customers look forward to the first Sunday in every month as 'car boot market day', and the task of getting enough cars to fill the site, costs of advertising, posters, etc. is kept to a minimum.

This is much more sensible and considerably more profitable than having car boot sales dotted about all over the place, at irregular intervals, and provoking the general response – 'not *another* car boot sale . . .'

SWOP SHOPS
Home-based swop shops are always great fun, and a most suitable alternative or adjunct to a jumble sale.

For the first one or two swop shops, limit your swoppers to a maximum of twenty or thirty, each paying a charge to bring their swops along. These can either be displayed at a central point, or in a separate room for swoppers to pick and choose what they are interested in. Or, to help the event along with smaller numbers, swoppers can take it in turns to list and show off their swops, with fellow swoppers ready to offer a fair exchange, including a cash transaction towards funds if there is any appreciable difference in value between the two items.

BRING-AND-BUY SALES
These used to be very popular when fund-raising was less sophisticated than it is now. Although this popularity does

seem to have waned somewhat, present-day fund-raisers are pleasantly surprised to discover that their fears of having an empty venue 'with nothing to sell and nobody bringing anything' – as one fund-raising friend put it – were completely unfounded.

If you do have any misgivings about such an event on an all-comers scale, try a mini bring-and-buy sale at home first, with invited guests bringing one thing and buying one thing. Charge an admission price and offer light refreshments. Then apply the same rule to a bring-and-buy sale as a public-based event, with customers delivering their offerings and donations as they enter.

Door money is a matter of choice here, although it is unlikely that any potential customer would object to a modest amount.

SECOND-HAND ROSE SHOWS
How often have you wailed aloud at the amount of clothes in good condition destined for the rag bag at the end of a jumble sale? Haven't we all!

Second-hand Rose fashion shows are a godsend for selling off good-as-new clothes which the jumble sale customers have missed, or which you might well be given by friends and relatives.

To begin with, sort out any clothes which you consider can go into the 'good as new' category, allowing for a minimum amount of mending, or quick dip in a washing machine, and classify them into types (e.g. coats, jackets, suits, dresses, nightwear and so on), and then into sizes.

Next task is to compile a list of possible models! Do not worry if these are a problem at first, because it usually takes just one adventurous soul for others in your group to look upon the whole event as a great joke, and volunteer to make their début gliding along the 'cat walk', in other words, between two groups of seating at your venue.

To attract interest, try including a headline in your publicity, such as 'NOTHING OVER £2'. Make admission by ticket only so that you can be sure you have adequate seating – although tickets can still be sold at the door on the day if need be.

Choose the very best clothes to be modelled – a maximum of twenty items, only – with a master or mistress of ceremonies (she is the one who will be called 'Second-hand Rose'!) detailing the fabric, colour, the sort of accessories the outfit can be worn with, and – most important – the size. Emphasise that the items modelled are just a few of the fashion selection on sale, and set up one or two booths for jewellery, scarves, bags and shoes, if you have enough.

Arrange changing areas with a good supply of tape measures, mirrors, etc. plus tea, coffee and biscuits for an interval break.

The secret is to keep closely to the idea of mannequins modelling clothes for film stars and celebrities in a large fashion house, paying particular attention to customer's needs, with an eye for detail. Convince your customers that buying second-hand can be just as rewarding and as enjoyable an experience for them too.

It works like a charm!

WASTE PAPER RE-CYCLING

The best possible use for all those out-of-date magazines at the end of any jumble sale! In fact, collecting waste paper has always been one of the most popular ways of raising funds, simply because there is always so much of it.

The snag, of course, is that waste paper takes up a lot of space, is heavy to handle, and has to be stored away from any fire risk, such as heaters or electrical wiring.

Begin by looking up *waste paper merchants* in the Yellow Pages and find out the minimum quantity which the nearest one will accept. This is likely to be one tonne.

Prices for waste paper vary from time to time, nevertheless it is an easy and regular source of revenue for many fund-raising groups, especially when funding a larger appeal.

ALUMINIUM CANS

Re-cycling aluminium fizzy drinks cans is fast becoming big business. So much so that there is now a special scheme in the U.K. approved by the Keep Britain Tidy group, whereby any fund-raising group can send off for a special 'Get You Started' package. This contains thirty special sacks, each one large enough to hold at least 200 crushed aluminium cans, posters and leaflets for collectors.

It can be a particularly good source of revenue when a fund-raising group works in close proximity to a bar, cafeteria or canteen! See appendix (4) (page 122) for details.

7

BOOST YOUR BAZAAR

The annual Christmas bazaar and/or summer fête is the highlight of any fund-raising year as well as the event which gives newcomers an insight into your fund-raising group, so it's important to give a good impression.

Start by choosing your date at least four or perhaps even six months in advance, so that there is no big panic about booking a hall, garden or field, getting prizes for raffles and sideshows, finding enough helpers to man the stalls, and getting organised.

Do not worry too much about your date clashing with another group's, unless it is an enormous and well-established event which will be well known throughout the neighbourhood. If in doubt, check with your local central library or council offices, to see what dates might be unsuitable locally.

As for national and international attractions on television, such as Wimbledon fortnight or test matches – well, if you wanted a completely uneventful weekend, then you'd most certainly be waiting for ever!

Here is an idea from a particularly inventive colleague who found that his son's school fête was to be held on the same Saturday as the Wimbledon final. He grabbed an empty classroom, installed a large colour television, persuaded his wife and daughter to serve strawberries and cream teas, and kept the room strictly out-of-bounds to anyone who had not paid 'ticket money' to watch the final in peace. And he charged other visitors a modest donation towards funds if they wanted to know the latest score!

Local tennis fans all agreed that their great day had been far more enjoyable than if they had been viewing at home with the threat of unexpected callers, telephone messages and all the other distractions. So there's nothing like a little bit of imagination to turn an unforeseen snag into a definite advantage . . .

A bazaar or fête has to be *entertaining*, a truly pleasurable way for people to enjoy themselves whilst spending money.

Aim for a complete programme of activities which will make your visitors want to stay and find out what is due to happen next. Darts competitions, sing-songs around a piano, cookery tasting . . . all attractions which can easily be set up for next to nothing, and which will add colour and interest.

Set aside a place for the tots and tinies – they get bored most easily and plead with mum to take them home. Section off a 'kiddies' corner' with old toys, dressing-up clothes, and perhaps a sand-tray and a paddling pool, if you can. At a modest hourly or half-hourly rate, most mothers will consider it a bargain. Have at least one adult on hand, and get each child's name, address and telephone number – self-stick labels on their fronts will do nicely.

Remember that older people do not always like walking or standing around for too long. Set groups of chairs around, especially near the refreshments bar or counter. The main reason why tea and biscuits *always* sell is not that people actually *want* to eat and drink, but so that they can stop for a break and a chat.

DON'T rely on the weather. Even if it isn't raining on the big day, a few indoor attractions (such as the old favourites 'housey-housey' or bingo, and 'treasure map', where people can pin different places on a map trying to guess where some 'treasure' prize might be hidden) always go down well.

Collect out-of-date magazines for people to browse through, and plan a display about the aims of the cause for which you are raising the money, to make your visitors even more interested.

Make out a list of stalls and possible attractions as early as you can. People are twice as likely to come along and help for some specific purpose – such as selling raffle tickets or manning the refreshments counter – than if some vague request is made where it is not clear what part they can expect to play.

Here is a list to check through:

REFRESHMENTS
The most important stall at any event! Quantities are always difficult to estimate, but you should budget in the proportion of six bottles or cartons of milk; one 125g packet of tea and a similar amount of instant coffee; two litre bottles of orange squash and a one litre bottle of lemon or grapefruit; and a ½kg or 1kg bag of sugar.

Make an appeal among your friends and supporters for biscuits and cakes, and buy potato crisps by the gross from your nearest confectionery wholesaler – address from your local business telephone directory.

Such wholesalers may also be good suppliers of cans of fizzy drinks – but be warned. Many smaller retail shops complain nowadays that the larger supermarkets are able to *sell* their canned fizzy drinks at a cheaper price than the wholesale price at which these retailers can *buy* – so do check prices first.

Aim for at least four helpers – two to serve customers, and two to wash, dry and tidy up.

HOME BAKES/HOME PRODUCE

Cakes, jams, biscuits, home-made sweets and candies . . . this is usually the stall which is sold out first! So the more produce you have the better.

BOOKS

Never in short supply. Discard any which are badly stained, warped, or falling apart.

PLANTS

Not only actual plants, but also cuttings, seeds, dried flower arrangements, flower pictures, unwanted plastic and paper varieties and nosegays or posies of wild flowers.

Most nurseries will also do a 'sale or return' deal, whereby fund-raising groups can keep the retail profit on any plants which are sold, and the rest returned after the bazaar or fête.

LUCKY DIPS

Keep dips cheap and cheerful, wrapped in remnants of giftwrap, tissue or scraps of wallpaper. 100 – 150 dips is generally about right, and if stocks seem to be short nearer the day, you can always buy a gross of cheap sweets from the nearest confectionery wholesaler.

TOMBOLA

Absolutely *anything* will do as prizes for this stall – from a can of furniture polish to a fairy doll! So if the tombola stall is still doing brisk business when the prizes on display are dwindling, re-stock from other stalls. Aim for 200 prizes per 1,000 raffle tickets. Attach the tear-off tickets with numbers ending in 0 or 5 to the prizes, and destroy the rest, keeping *all* the counterfoils. These are then folded and put into a

drum or container for the lucky customers to pay their money
and see if they can pull out a winning number. Who knows
what they might be taking home?

FORTUNE TELLING

Another *very* popular attraction – as I know to my cost when
I stagger home with an aching back and a sore throat as the
very last person to pack up and go home! But if you are not
fortunate enough to have a palmist or crystal-ball-gazer in
your group, still have someone dressed up as an old gypsy to
'read' tea-leaves near the refreshment tent. Or type out and
photocopy a stock of imaginary horoscopes or zodiac character analyses, ready to be sold from a decorated basket – just
like gypsies at fairgrounds and race meetings used to do.

TODDLERS' TOGS

Another spin-off from your last jumble sale. Top it up with
donations from committee members, most of whom are
almost sure to have children and grandchildren who always
seem to be growing out of their clothes. Aim for just one or
two prices to cover all items.

BOTTLE STALL

Do you know – it is absolutely amazing the number of things
one can find in bottles. Not only bottles – but jars, glasses,
screw-top containers . . . in fact, almost anything made of
glass. So, well before the big day, get all committee members
and their friends to collect all they can, particularly baby food
containers which always look so pretty and dainty with their
lids painted over with household enamel, shoe dye or nail
varnish. (Very useful for making a colourful display on the
gift stall too.)

Wines and spirits are always crowd-pullers at the bottle
stall, which makes it worthwhile approaching off-licences,
supermarkets and wine merchants for suitable donations. But
humbler items, such as tomato ketchup, ink, shampoo, vin-
egar and salad cream are also worth winning, with varying
quantities of tea, coffee, spices and sugar in jars.

You can run your bottle stall along the same lines as the
tombola. Or, for a change, you could use two packs of playing
cards, with Kings, Queens, Jacks and Aces as the lucky cards
to win a bottle prize.

SANTA CLAUS

Tackle Santa's sack gifts in the same way as the lucky dip.
Explore the possibility of hiring his costume from another

fund-raising group, department store, or fancy dress hire firm.

The idea of Santa's grotto may be very appealing to adults, but the prospect of venturing into the unknown is often very frightening to a small child. See fig. 3 for our plan of an easily constructed sleigh and/or throne instead, and make room for a sparkly Christmas tree nearby, with fairy lights and little sweet-treats.

(a)

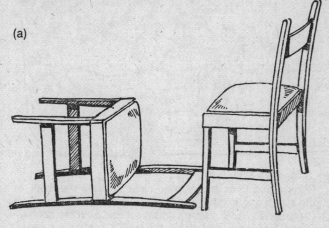

(b)

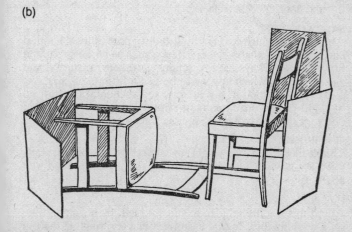

(c)

Fig. 3. Santa's Sleigh.
(a) Constructed from an upturned chair to make the 'boot' of the sleigh and another chair for Santa's seat.
(b) Place cardboard cut from cartons around both the chairs.
(c) Cover the chairs and cardboard with Christmassy paper, tinsel, etc. and fill the hollow of the upturned chair with toys and packets for a lucky dip.

FANCY GOODS
Another title which covers a multitude of possibilities! Knitted and embroidered goods; craft items, such as baskets, painted flower pots (always a good seller), jewellery, pictures, and any donations which appear to be just a little bit special. At one Christmas bazaar, my younger son's school was surprised by a gift of two dozen pairs of false eyelashes, but they sold out very quickly indeed under the 'fancy goods' banner!

SIDESHOWS
Things like 'guess the weight' of a cake, or box of groceries, keep the crowds happy, just as long as they are spaced well apart.

HOOPLA
Adapt this traditional idea to suit yourself, by pegging prizes on a washing line, so that customers can try 'ringing' the top

of the peg with a hoop cut from a yoghourt tub or circular slices from a washing-up liquid bottle, as shown in fig. 4.

Fig. 4. Hoopla.
Peg prizes to a washing line. The hoops must ring over the top of the pegs.

FISHING

Fishing for plastic ducks with 'lucky numbers' or 'lucky names' on the underside is another firm favourite. Or you could use the same idea with fish cut from sheets of polystyrene packing, which you could probably get for nothing from a local shop. So simple to set up, with the help of a paddling pool or baby bath, with loops of fuse wire and some off-cuts of dowelling or cane from a do-it-yourself shop. See fig 5 (overleaf).

Simply thread about 15cm (6 inches) of fuse wire (both ends) through a fish cut-out, making holes with a stout darning needle, and securing the underside with putty or plasticine. Similarly, for each fishing rod, stick both ends of a 15cm (6 inch) length of fuse wire into a piece of putty or plasticine, then wedge this into one end of the cane or dowelling, bending the double thickness end into a hook shape.

PICK-A-STRAW

This is another quick and easy sideshow to set up, because all you need is a square peg-board, and a bag of ordinary drinking straws.

Cut each straw in half so that you have approximately 100 – 120 pieces. Cut the same number of small slips of paper, and write 'prize', or the value of coins if you want to keep to money prizes, on between 40 and 50 of these. Then roll up your entire supply of paper slips and stick them into the ends of the straws, so that some are 'blank' and some are winners, and insert them into the peg-board at random, 'filled end' first. Especially popular with the children!

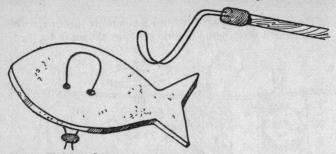

Fig. 5. Fishing Game.
For the fish: Cut out a fish shape from polystyrene, thread a
length of fuse wire through it to make a loop, securing the ends
with plasticine.
For the fishing rod: Stick both ends of a length of fuse wire into
the end of a piece of dowelling and secure with putty or plasticine.
Bend the double length of fuse wire into a hook shape and then
you are ready for fishing!

BEACH-COMBING
A couldn't-be-simpler sideshow, this one, with children in
mind – although mums and senior citizens have been known
to enjoy a bit of beach-combing in miniature on the quiet!

You need a fairly deep sand tray, just large enough to fit
on top of a desk or table. A shallow supermarket carton lined
inside and out with discarded plastic carrier bags will do. Get
a vegetable colander or a riddle, a small supply of paper cups
and a handful of assorted coins and small trinkets.

Throw the coins and trinkets into the sand, and give it a
good rake over, so that everything is hidden. Customers then
pay for a turn with a paper cup which they fill with sand in
the hopes of some 'treasure' when it is sieved through the
colander or riddle.

PLAY YOUR CARDS RIGHT
An idea shamelessly filched from a popular UK television
show! And all you need is a pack of extra-large playing cards.
These can be hand-printed on to cards cut to shape, from art
suppliers or craft shops. 15cm × 21cm is a good size. As long
as the suit and value of each card is easily recognisable, that's
really all that matters!

You will also need a fairly large piece of plywood or
hardboard – about 80cm by 80cm – and pin or tack lengths

Fig. 6. Play Your Cards Right.
Pin or nail lengths of cheap battening across a length of plywood
or hardboard so that cards can be placed into position. Place
the board on an easel or lean it against a wall or chair.

of battening across this widthways. Place the board on an
easel (like a blackboard) – and your attraction is all ready for
its first customer.

The stall-holder or helper will deal out fifteen cards – three
rows of five – across the battening, face down. The first card
is turned over, then the customer has to guess whether the
next card is higher or lower in value. If they succeed in this
across the first row, then they double the money paid to try

their luck on this game. And if they are successful in correctly predicting 'higher' or 'lower' to the last card on the board, then they win four times their money.

Highly profitable for the organiser!

DARTS

There are many ways of arranging a darts sideshow. It depends on how many prizes you can offer. If these are in plentiful supply and on a small scale, then you can set a score for dart throwers such as thirty or over (for three darts). Or you can seal various amounts of cash in small envelopes, ready to be pinned on to a piece of hardboard, and colour in one corner of each envelope for the dart throwers to hit and win the money inside.

Alternatively, for a slightly different type of darts competition, you might like to offer three prizes for the best three scores of the afternoon, with perhaps a booby prize for the lowest score, and a special set of prizes for the ladies and children who do not generally score as high as the gentlemen.

GOLFER'S HANDICAP

Spread a length of plastic sheeting (or similar) on the ground and pin down as tightly as possible. Then stick or pin a currency note, gift voucher or 'free go' ticket for another bazaar or fête attraction (or any combination of all three!) at one end. Have a golf ball at the other end.

Each would-be golfer has to try and putt the ball on to the paper prize in order to win. This is not as easy as it looks, but is very quick to set up, and often a matter of pride to budding golf champions.

The distance between the golf ball and paper prize does not really matter, because a short putt is often just as difficult as a long shot. But get a regular golf player to work out a reasonable length if you still aren't too sure after a few practice shots yourself.

CASH CASCADE

The very last sideshow involving water, but one which is so easy to introduce that it seems unjust to leave out! Fill a bucket with water and sink a one pound coin to the bottom. Then your customers can drop 10ps in the bucket, trying their best to get one directly over the pound. If they succeed in covering the pound completely – and I have never seen it done yet! – then they win not only the pound, but all the other money in the bucket. You can safely offer a free go if they even get it to touch the pound.

SKITTLES

Another sideshow which is easily set up and dismantled and always a fair crowd-puller. If funds do not allow the purchase of children's skittles, a dozen or so plastic lemonade bottles will not break the budget. Put a few drips of household enamel paint into an empty bottle, replace the screw cap and shake for a brightly coloured nine-pin. You can use a different colour for each skittle or put in lots of different colours, swishing them round one at a time, for a multi-colour effect.

The runway needs to be approximately 11 – 12 feet long. You can allow 3 balls per 12 skittles and award prizes on a scale from 5 to 9 skittles knocked over.

SPORTS

Have you ever thought about setting up a cricket match or five-a-side football game? The teams will enjoy the sport even more than winning a prize and you can charge spectators to watch!

And if you want to raise funds from sports players, why not rig up a net, get yourself a largish ball and charge for a half-hour practice game of volleyball? It's an ideal game for this type of event, being easy to learn and able to be played either between two players or up to ten or twelve.

Netball, basketball, roller-skating (bring your own skates) and skateboarding for the boys and girls are all good possibilities, using the same idea.

DEMONSTRATIONS

These are not meant to be money-spinners in themselves, but will give your visitors a good reason both to visit your bazaar or fête and to stay and see what is going on.

Contact the road safety officer of your local council. (The nearest public library will be pleased to help you if you are not too sure how to go about this.) He or she will advise you on getting a road safety display going and might contribute things like charts, stickers and funny hats. Road safety officers are always keen on helping young cyclists, so you could invite people to bring their machines along for an expert check-up, as well as hints on security and guarding against damage and theft.

First aid organisations, animal welfare groups, craft clubs, drama societies, charity organisations, dance and music clubs – they are all usually interested in becoming known to a wider public. It is up to you and your fund-raising colleagues to make the first approach.

Addresses from the entertainment department or information desk of your local authority or arts council!

COMMERCIAL FIRMS AND SMALL BUSINESSES

A lady colleague on one fund-raising group noticed – as we all had – that a number of building societies were making concerted efforts in the national press and on T.V. to woo young savers, with free money boxes, carrier bags and stickers.

Off she went to the nearest office, approached the desk, introduced herself and asked whether they would be interested in running a stall at a forthcoming Christmas bazaar at a charge which, she correctly guessed, was equivalent to their fortnightly milk bill.

Back came the answer within a matter of days – yes. The building society would be most interested and the assistant manager himself would come along to man the stall, bringing with him armfuls of give-away money boxes, stickers and other goodies.

Twenty new junior savers accounts were opened at that bazaar with a few more afterwards, as a result of Christmas pocket money and seasonal bonuses. Needless to say, that building society is now a regular feature, beloved by fund-raisers for the extra revenue it brings in and by the children and parents who are always delighted to get something for nothing.

There really is no harm in asking. And if an organisation or business concern is not interested, then at least they will know about your fund-raising efforts and that might well encourage them to give some type of support on another occasion.

Are there any 'home visit' hairdressers or beauty specialists in your area? Look in the 'personal' or 'services' columns of your local paper.

Hair-cutting, manicures and facials are sure to prove an added attraction, with takings shared on an agreed percentage basis and the visitors able to decorate a small pitch in any way they like, in order to advertise their services. And there is no better advertisement than letting potential customers see the standard of workmanship!

Here are a few other suggestions for this part of your bazaar or fête:

INSURANCE COMPANIES – particularly car insurance, which is a most competitive business these days.

FANCY DRESS HIRE SHOPS – extremely popular at Hallowe'en and Christmas.

HIRE SERVICES – of all kinds, especially those connected with do-it-yourself, gardening and household maintenance – all suitable for the family audience at a fête or bazaar.

UPHOLSTERERS – equipped with fabric samples and colour schemes.

HOME IMPROVEMENTS – double-glazing, cladding, wrought iron works, landscape gardening, etc. etc.

DANCE STUDIOS – especially if they can combine some sort of display to tempt children and/or adults!

DISCO ORGANISERS – chance of some expert (and free!) background music here!

CAKE DECORATORS – always popular, but especially during the pre-Christmas period and for summer weddings.

COMPUTER STOCKISTS AND SPECIALISTS

CRAFT AND HOBBY SHOPS

PRIVATE TUITION SPECIALISTS

DRIVING SCHOOLS

WEDDING SPECIALISTS

THE MASTER PLAN

About three months before the event, work through each section of your bazaar programme – i.e. stalls, sideshows, sports and demonstrations – and draw up a list of helpers, along with any preferences as to what they would like to do.

Taking an average of around 25 attractions – more of course, with a large venue and extra helpers – and your programme could read something like this:

REFRESHMENTS plus another 10 – 12 stalls
RAFFLE plus between 5 – 6 sideshows
2 DEMONSTRATIONS and/or VISITING STALLS
2 GAMES and/or SPORTS DISPLAYS

Do not forget to allocate at least two people to take door or gate money – most important and often overlooked!

Once you have drawn up your list of attractions and 'pen-

cilled in' helpers on paper, it is worth inspecting the venue,
even if you feel you know it well. Check on all facilities, such
as fire exits, toilets, wash basins, running water, car parking
etc. Also make a note to bring some spare kitchen paper
towelling, soap and rolls of toilet paper. These always seem
to run out at the last minute.

Two of you should arm yourselves with a packet of chalk,
duster, pencil and paper, and mark off where each proposed
attraction is to go, making a rough diagram at the same time.
Copy this on to a fairly large sheet of paper afterwards so
that everyone knows where to position themselves.

See if there is any spare space for additional attractions,
another sideshow, or easily erected game, such as skittles or
beach-combing.

Only one cautionary note at this stage.

Don't plan your stalls around the hall, leaving a gaping
square in the middle. Customers feel so vulnerable walking
into an empty area, especially at the beginning of an event.
It is a fairly speedy matter to arrange a few groups of chairs
around small tables with 'PLEASE HELP YOURSELF' notices
for magazines. This area can always be thinned out and chairs
removed if crowds are a problem.

The idea of a celebrity being invited to come and perform
an opening ceremony may be suggested – but you have to
remember that even the most co-operative and friendly of
T.V. or stage personality can only come and open your bazaar
or fête if he or she does not receive a booking for work at
the last minute. Anyway, whomever you invite may work
almost exclusively for one or two pet charities and good causes
of their own, as many stars do.

Many such personalities only work through an agent who
will negotiate the fee, which may be high even though you
are a worthy cause!

Instead of a celebrity, it might be better to have a 'theme'
to your event, with a suitable character or characters to open
the proceedings, along with simple 'give-aways' for customers
at the opening ceremony. For instance, my husband is always
very popular as the 'cuddly Father Christmas' who opens my
son's school Christmas bazaar by throwing sweeties to the
children and visitors as he proceeds to the Christmas tree,
with Christmas carols and other touches of seasonal cheer to
complete the Christmas theme. It *always* pays to introduce a

theme for spring fayres and summer fêtes too, to help customers remember your group before and after the event, as well as lending a little more interest and giving a certain touch of distinction. Here are some examples:

TRAMPS AND RAGAMUFFINS
This is a very easy theme to follow, because all the 'costumes' can be rescued from the rag-bag or jumble sale leavings, with blackened teeth, painted warts and freckles!

To be opened by – 'Gorzel Wummidge'
Free give-aways – 'crusts' (fingers) of previously toasted bread and butter

HOME FARM
So easy to forget that almost every inner city area was once farmland, if one can go back far enough. Hunt out roomy shirts and nightdresses to make smocks for the ladies, to be worn with mob-caps, scarves and shawls; and trousers tied at the knees and ankles to make gaiters, with straw hats or trilbies for the gentlemen.

To be opened by – Farmer (name of group)
Free give-aways – slices of apple

VILLAGE MARKET
Another 'days gone by' theme, which always works perfectly, because stall-holders can dress in the costume of almost any era, from mediaeval maidens to Victorian damsels and muffin men. Rescue bridesmaids' dresses and wedding parasols from the loft and trim the ankles of pyjamas with ribbon or braid to make Victorian pantalettes for little girls! Additional attractions such as puppet shows, wandering minstrels and jousting contests.

To be opened by – the town crier
Free give-aways – duplicated shopping lists

LAND OF NURSERY RHYME
Lots of characters and ideas to choose from here, with nobody likely to be stuck for inspiration! Everyone has their own image of what nursery time favourites such as Miss Muffet,

Boy Blue, Bo Peep and Jack Horner would have looked like, it is usually a question of bringing in accessories to make each character recognisable – a plastic spider dangling from elastic on a stick for Miss Muffet; a 'shepherd's crook' for Bo Peep; a toy trumpet for Boy Blue and a pie for Jack Horner.

To be opened by – the nursery rhyme parade
Free give-aways – sweeties

ORANGES AND LEMONS
Just one example of a spin-off idea – this one from the 'nursery rhyme' theme, using the 'oranges and lemons' rhyme to inspire a colour scheme of orange and lemon, with all stall-holders wearing clothes in orange and lemon, and stalls decorated to match.

To be opened by – Mr Orange and Mrs Lemon
Free give-aways – orange segments or sweets

LAND OF TOYS
Dolls, soldiers, teddies, bunnies – each one sure to attract customers, both young and old.

To be opened by – Mr Edward Bear
Free give-aways – sweets and/or biscuits

KINGS AND QUEENS
Here again, lots of scope for anyone with just a sprinkling of imagination – from a fictional monarch such as Old King Cole to the Tudors and Stuarts, or any other realm you like to think of.

To be opened by – the Queen of Hearts
Free give-aways – miniature jam tarts

CLOWN CAVALCADE
Yet another idea which is easy to follow! A reasonable supply of make-up or greasepaint and the costumes will usually suggest themselves without any bother – the more ridiculous the better!

To be opened by – those famous clowns – Wibble and Wobble

Free give-aways – wobbly jelly in spoons or mini jam-pots

MAGIC AND MYSTERY
This is another 'anything goes' category. Conjurors (costumes only remember!); witches, wizards, sorcerers; goblins; show-girls, etc.

To be opened by – Il Great Magico
Free give-aways – invitations to some sort of magic show or magical presentation, as part of the proceedings

HAPPY FAMILIES
Mr Bun the baker, Mrs Bone the butcher's wife, Miss Stamp the postman's daughter, Master Wood, the carpenter's son – you could meet them all at a 'happy families' fête, with a special prize for the first visitor correctly to challenge all four members of one family by visiting different stalls and getting a lucky programme signed with the autographs of each correctly challenged member of a happy family!

To be opened by – Mr Bun the baker
Free give-aways – 'free go' tickets

AROUND THE WORLD
What limits are there here? You could have children in Red Indian and cowboy costumes. Spanish Señoritas in plain black dresses with combs in their hair. Indian ladies in sarees. Eskimo lads in boots and anoraks . . . the list is endless! A good idea for a multi-racial area and in any situation where there is scope for people to bring along their own outfits.

To be opened by – the world fairy
Free give-aways – snacks and tit-bits offered by those taking part, on their stalls

Deciding on a particular theme for your fête or bazaar will also make it easier to decorate sideshows and stalls. Drape a stall (as shown on page 44) whenever possible – not only to disguise any untidy patches, but also to discourage pilfering . . . sad but true, it does happen at all too many fund-raising events.

Use boldly-coloured cut-outs from greeting cards,

wallpaper, gift wrapping – anything you can get hold of – stuck on to cardboard for extra strength and either pinned or stuck around the stall and on to your drapes.

Coloured plastic bags are another good source of free decoration, particularly effective for cutting out coloured shapes, streamers and bunting. Simply cut across widthways, cut one seam, then fold concertina fashion across the whole length and cut whatever shape you like.

One or two stalls can be canopied or given a fascia in order to give varying heights and make the overall effect more interesting and pleasing to the eye.

Lengths of battening can be pinned or tacked to the sides of the stalls or tables, so that you can drape them as you wish, or use them for hanging banners or bunting. Or, if this is not practical, try sinking two broom handles or garden canes into buckets of sand or soil at either side of the stall to support a banner (see fig. 7).

(a)

(b)

Fig. 7. To decorate and vary the height of stalls.
(a) Pin or tack lengths of battening to the edges of tables and
    sides of stalls, then drape with bunting and/or balloons.
(b) Sink broom handles into buckets of sand or soil, then drape
    across the top with a banner or bunting.

However – do not treat every stall in the same way. It will
defeat the purpose of giving each stall a different appeal of
its own, add to your precious preparation time and take up
extra space into the bargain!

THE PROGRAMME

The next job is to plan your bazaar or fête programme, to
raise more money for your group.

Check our easy-to-follow lay-out and you will see how to
set out all your attractions on one page, then divide up the
remaining pages into spaces which you can then sell to private
advertisers. Our programme should give you clues as to the
type of small business you should approach.

Ask committee members to approach shops and businesses which they patronise, from supermarkets to slimmers' clubs – if not for advertising space, then for a gift or donation.

Local employers are another good source of support, particularly if committee members are among the work-force.

Either make a personal approach, or write a letter – e.g.:

Dear Mr Smith

Old Chapel Senior Citizen's Club will be holding a Christmas bazaar on November 20th at St John's Hall, Northway, to raise money for the new work-room and extension appeal.

As a member of the appeal committee, I am taking the liberty of writing to ask if you could very kindly spare any of your company's products for us to use as a raffle or sideshow prize. If this is not possible, we should be most grateful for any kind of donation, large or small.

We very much hope that you will feel able to support us in this venture, which we are sure will benefit many elderly people in our neighbourhood for years to come.

When replying, perhaps you could also indicate whether or not you require any acknowledgement of your gift, either on our programme, or by announcement at the bazaar.

Many thanks for giving this your consideration.

Yours sincerely

MAKE A TIME-TABLE

Lastly – just to make quite sure that nothing is overlooked or forgotten! – here is a time-table for your bazaar or fête, which you may find helpful to copy and circulate to all your committee members and helpers.

FOUR MONTHS or even up to SIX MONTHS before the event

Book your venue and begin a list of possible helpers. Start collecting baby-food jars, and hangers for clothes. Work out a budget for expenditure to include advertising, posters and refreshments, adding a further amount for small items such as raffle tickets, toilet rolls, etc. Then you can decide on a proportional rate for outside stall-holders. Book essentials such as marquees, equipment etc.

Otterbridge Special School

for Mentally Handicapped Children

CHRISTMAS BAZAAR

Saturday 8th November

at

OTTERBRIDGE SCHOOL

Ash Road, Otterbridge
2 p.m. until 5 p.m.
programme

15p

REGISTERED CHARITY NO. 123456

Fig. 8. Example Programme (front page).

BARGAIN STALLS

Tombola   Books   Records

Home Bakes   Raffles Stall

Plants   Palm Reading   Toys

Handicrafts   Lucky Dip

Hand Writing Analysis

Pick-A-Straw   Toddlers Togs

Nearly New Clothing

White Elephant   Greetings Cards

Games   Jumble

Refreshments

ETC. ETC. ETC.

Fig. 8. Example Programme (page 2).

A CUT ABOVE

Unisex Hair Fashions
3 High Street, Otterbridge
Tel: 83220

DAVID'S

1 Hawthorn Way,
Otterbridge

Sub Post Office
★ Tobacconist ★
Newsagent
(Newspapers delivered)

Tel: 28302

BTM

Biggs's Timber Merchants
5 Station Road, Otterbridge, Tel: 23820

Lady Jane

LADIES' FASHION WEAR
9 High Street, Otterbridge
Telephone: 20328

2 Station Road, Otterbridge, Tel: 80322
Come to
SUNSHINE AIRWAYS
for bargain breaks

Fig. 8. Example Programme (page 3).

MARTIN'S BAKERY

Crusty bread & rolls

WHOLESALE & RETAIL

Wedding cakes our speciality!

Woodside Way, Otterbridge * * * Tel: 30282

★THE FRUIT SHOP★

Wholesale – Retail – Cash & Carry

4 High Street, Otterbridge Tel: 20238

THE ADVENTURE CENTRE

Sells: Golf/Football/Bowling/Windsurfing/ Canoeing & Camping Gear

PLUS MUCH MORE

4 Marine Terrace, Otterbridge (Tel: 80223)

SMITH & CO (Glaziers)

for all your D·I·Y needs • Glass cut while you wait

7 High Street, Otterbridge Tel: 32208

LUCKY PROGRAMME SLIP

(Fill in and give to the gate steward.)

Name ....

Address ....

.... Tel: ....

Fig. 8. Example Programme (back page).

THREE MONTHS before the event
Draw up a list of *possible* attractions and continue list of helpers. No fund-raising group can have too many!

Begin approaching families and friends for gifts and donations.

Ask committee members to list possible donors and benefactors among shops and businesses whom they patronise.

Approach potential outside stall-holders (remember to ask for a small deposit when booking a stall or pitch).

Decide on a suitable theme.

Check on any free advertising in programmes of community events, 'What's On' free newsletters and entries in local newspapers.

TWO MONTHS before the event
Time for an inspection visit to your venue, in order to check on fire exits and toilets and introduce your group to the caretaker.

Compile a chart for stall-holders.

Complete list for all outside stall-holders.

Check whether any tables need to be hired – as is so often the case – and make the necessary arrangements.

SIX WEEKS before the event
All letters appealing for raffle and sideshow prizes should have been sent by now!

Send in free advertisements for local community programmes and free newsletters and get permission to display posters in any public places, such as libraries, health centres etc.

Plan lay-out for fête or bazaar programme, including advertising space and list possible advertisers/printers to approach.

ONE MONTH before the event
Make this your one-month deadline for all advertising space to be sold so that advertisements can be drawn up, lettered and approved by the advertisers, with money promised – or, better still! – collected.

Make a final list of helpers and check on collection of prizes for raffle and sideshows, making a further appeal in local newspapers and among supporters if need be.

Get posters drawn up and duplicated, ready to be coloured in.

Check advertisement rates for local newspapers.

THREE WEEKS before the event
Check prices for refreshment items, particularly fizzy drinks.

Compile press advertisements and distribute posters.

Ask all stall-holders to make sure of their costumes, stall decorations, etc. and allocate prizes.

TWO WEEKS before the event
Send in any press information to local newspapers. Make any repairs which may be necessary to banners, bunting, etc. replenish stocks and type out publicity slips, if needed.

TEN DAYS before the event
Send in advertisements to local newspapers.
Contact local radio stations with news items.
Begin selling advance programmes.
Check provision for background music at the event.

SEVEN DAYS before the event
Make a last check on stalls, helpers and – most important – transportation of both goods and helpers to your venue on the day itself.

TWO DAYS before the event
Distribute half the quantity of publicity slips, via letter-boxes near venue.
Purchase all necessary items for refreshments.

ON THE DAY
Erect banners, bunting, arrow-pointers, and equip sandwich-board men to hand publicity slips to shoppers.

Station the two biggest, strongest helpers at the gate to collect entrance money!

And may all your profits be great ones!

8

MONEY SPINNERS

Events such as the summer fête, Christmas bazaar and twice-yearly jumble sale are familiar, but their ever-popular public appeal means that they are seen as a main source of income in themselves, rather than highlights in a programme of events for people to enjoy all the year round.

Every year we see a flurry of Christmas fayres and bazaars, followed by long weeks and months when nothing much seems to be happening, until the first promise of June sunshine heralds the start of the summer fête season. And that's a shame – because there's nothing like a friendly square dance to cheer up the dull days of winter, just as a leisurely afternoon tea lends a particularly tranquil note to the start of spring.

Or what about a barn dance as part of harvest celebrations; or afternoon tea, complete with hot toast and buttered muffins, on a frosty January afternoon? All the fund-raising ideas in this chapter are strictly 'non-seasonal' ones which you can slot into any existing programme.

PROFIT MARGIN!
Work out how much you need to spend out before trying to calculate how much money will come in!

First, list all costs i.e. –

1) hire of hall,
2) catering budget,
3) cost of prizes,
4) price of printed tickets, and
5) any special costs given in the following information for each fund-raising event, such as the fee for a square dance 'caller'.

The total costs involved should indicate the profit which you can expect to make. As a general principle, you should multiply total costs by three, then divide this figure by the number of tickets you realistically expect to sell, to arrive at the admission charge. Extra profits will derive from the raffle and licensed bar etc.

CHOOSING A VENUE

Many very entertaining events can be staged at home! But for large-scale occasions – for example, craft fairs and music halls – you will need to hire a hall.

Unless you have an obvious choice, such as a parish building or community centre, contact the lettings department of your local council and ask for a list of council-maintained halls (such as schools, technical colleges and sports centres) which are available for hire, and the charges. Mid-week hire is usually cheaper than Friday evenings and week-ends. And if you are associated with any particular school, it could well be that you are entitled to free use of the hall at certain times, if you ask.

However, a free venue must *not* mean super-cheap tickets, because if you *do* have to pay hire charges at a future occasion, and allow for these in your ticket price, the next event will seem far too expensive.

So allow for a venue hire charge even if there isn't one.

Enquire about facilities for car parking and access by public transport as well.

CATERING

Refreshments, snack lunches, ploughmen's suppers etc. all increase the admission charge.

Buffets or serve-yourself meals pose a problem when estimating quantities – mainly because one type of sandwich *always* proves to be more popular than the rest! But two and a half slices of bread (brown or white) per person is fairly safe overall, that is ten sliced loaves per hundred guests.

Choose simple fillings, such as egg mayonnaise (hard-boiled eggs chopped and mashed with a little mayonnaise or salad cream), cheese, pâté or ham. 'Fishy' smells from the buffet table soon pervade the air if sardine or fish-paste sandwiches aren't eaten at a brisk pace, although the more delicate aroma of salmon makes this a much safer fish filling.

PLOUGHMEN'S SUPPERS

These may take just a little longer to prepare and transport to your venue. But 'supper time' is always greeted with wholehearted enthusiasm and they are so much easier to calculate accurately.

For a costing for one hundred people (all prices correct at the time of going to press), please refer to appendix (5), page 123.

BARS

A bar is an attraction at events, particularly in the evenings and at week-ends. So treat this as a completely separate profit centre. See appendix (6), page 123, for how to get a licence.

Off-licences will generally be pleased to stock your bar with a variety of drinks on sale or return and may lend glasses as well. Don't forget soft drinks. Wine should be sold for about double what it costs (a standard 75cl bottle gives six glasses). This makes quite a handsome profit, though you cannot make such a good mark-up on beer.

ADVERTISING

Very necessary to attract the general public – but not much usually required for a home-based event where you don't want to be crowded out of the kitchen. Refer to Chapter 5, 'Spread the Word Around' (page 35), and adapt the suggestions to suit your occasion.

TICKETS

These can be printed or duplicated/photocopied. They represent a receipt for the admission charge which many people like to have.

You will find that the cost of *printed* tickets can vary enormously from one place to another, so it is worth shopping around and getting quotes from different printers and print shops.

TEA-PARTIES

Do you remember the days of 'afternoon tea' when the table was laid with wafer-thin bread and butter, cucumber sandwiches, sponge fingers, fruit cake, biscuits and scones?

It seems a delightful novelty now, which may be the reason

why cafés and restaurants offering afternoon teas attract such unrivalled custom.

From a fund-raising point of view, the best thing about entertaining visitors to afternoon tea is that it need cost absolutely NOTHING (providing, of course, that teas, coffees and home-bakes can be donated) and can usually be arranged at fairly short notice.

The most important tradition of afternoon tea was always that people *sat down* together, rather than wandering around and chatting cup-in-hand. So you may have to think about borrowing extra chairs or arranging deck-chairs and sun loungers outside if the weather is fine.

Keep the number of invitations down to a maximum of around twenty-five people to start with, so that you learn how to plan your party in true tea-time style. Small card-tables are ideal, or you may like to use a wall-papering table draped with white sheeting.

The main thing is to keep to an 'afternoon tea' theme, with table-cloths, little vases or pots of flowers (pretty margarine tubs and plastic bases from lemonade bottles make lovely centre-pieces), doily-covered plates, and real cups and saucers, if you have enough to go around, rather than mugs or disposable beakers.

For approximately twenty-five people you will find that half a 125g packet of tea is enough for two cups per guest and you should only need one lemon for those who enjoy lemon tea and two pints of milk – served in milk-jugs, of course!

Supporters are usually willing to supply small quantities of tea-time dainties, such as scones, fairy cakes, biscuits and those thin-cut sandwiches which we all love and remember! Packets of savoury crackers from the supermarket also provide a good base for pâté or cheese spreads, garnished with thin slices of tomato, gherkin or cucumber to add colour to your tea-table.

Base your charges on the more modest café or snack bar prices and you are sure to find plenty of customers among your own fund-raising circle, especially if you invite them to bring along their own friends and neighbours. And, for non tea-drinkers, you could have one or two jugs of fruit squash, suitably garnished.

The ideal 'tea-time' is around 3 pm – 5 pm, and you will soon discover that the school holiday periods are particularly popular, when hard-pressed mums and grans can come along for tea and a chat. The children can have their own tea-party, with plenty of toys, drinks and crisps, outside, or in another room!

Variations on a theme
CHEESE AND WINE PARTIES for evening get-togethers are an especially economical proposition nowadays, when wine is cheaper in real terms than ever before, or indeed anyone can make quite a respectable range of wines from the selection of home-brew kits on sale at budget-beating prices. The wine should not be *sold*; this would be illegal.

Add cheese rolls, cheese savouries, cheese biscuits, cheese crisps and cheese dips to make plain cheese go further.

BARBECUES have become a very popular fund-raiser in recent years, particularly with the advent of easy-to-use home barbecue accessories.

Allow three or four food items per person – such as a chicken leg or wing, sausage, jacket potato and hamburger – with an allowance of French bread or rolls and serve-yourself salad. Remember to allow costings for barbecue charcoal and incidentals such as paper napkins, plates, skewers, etc. If large numbers are expected, then cooking facilities need to be on a *very* large scale, or else it will take a long time to serve everybody.

Do make provision for a rainy or cloudy day by hiring a marquee or tents, perhaps from a local Scout troop or first aid group.

PICK-A-DISH
This can either be a fund-raising event in itself, or an extra attraction on an occasion such as afternoon tea, when a raffle might seem rather out of place.

The idea is to ask between ten and twenty friends and supporters each to provide a dish which can be served as one course in a meal. This means you could have anything from an attractive green salad to a savoury dip, or cakes or trifle to a flan or tart.

Or you may like to stick to pastry-based dishes so that your cooks can choose to create a savoury such as cheese and tomato quiche or a traditional pudding like treacle tart. 'Sweet and savoury' is always a very attractive 'pick-a-dish' theme.

All the dishes should be displayed on a table, together with a little pot or box beside each one, plus slips of paper and an array of pens and pencils. Guests are then invited to bid for any dish which takes their fancy by writing down their name and the amount of their bid, folding it and putting it into the pot or box. At the end of the proceedings, each pot is emptied and the highest bid is the one which buys each dish.

Variation on a theme
'HUSH-HUSH' AUCTIONS are great fun with items of bric-a-brac and 'nearly-new' clothing being sold by tender instead of food dishes – an added attraction with a difference for larger events – and no raffle tickets to sell either!

QUIZ EVENING
This event works best for around a hundred people, so you will need to hire a hall, with an admission charge to include either a buffet meal or ploughman's supper.

Each fund-raiser or supporter brings along friends or acquaintances to make up a quiz team of ten people per table. You need a question master to set and ask the questions, plus at least one scrutineer to ensure fair play and to check the answers which will be handed in by the leader or spokesman from each team.

Once the question has been set by the question master, each team can confer as much as they please, for – say – half a minute, at the end of which time a bell is rung. (Kitchen timers are indispensable for this part of the proceedings!) By then, each team leader must have written down the answer on the direction of the team and handed in the slip of paper to the question master for marking.

The team with the highest number of correct answers at the end of the evening is the winner, each member receiving a modest prize, such as a bottle of champagne-cider. The team with the lowest score also wins a 'booby' prize, such as ten lollipops, tea bags or sticks of sea-side rock! Anything to raise a few smiles from the tables of non-prize winners.

As well as the hire charges for your hall, cost of ploughmen's suppers or buffet, allow for the cost of the quiz winners' prizes, but do have a raffle as an extra attraction for the interval.

BEETLE DRIVE

This is a fund-raising occasion which folk of all ages enjoy. All you need are some dice, little pads of paper and one pen or pencil per person.

A beetle drive can be as grand an affair or as cosy a get-together as you like to make it. So you could hold it in a garden or through-lounge just as well as in a church hall, with admission charges varying from a beetle drive with tea and biscuits, to one which includes an interval buffet and bar. And the general idea is easy enough for 'first timers' to follow too.

Small tables are set around to seat four people apiece, with partners facing each other. Players take it in turns to throw the die, and the one with the highest score starts the drive, play then proceeding clockwise round the table. The object is for each pair to complete drawing their beetle before the other pair does so.

Either partner must throw a six to begin, by drawing the beetle's body. Then, either partner needs to throw a five before the beetle's head can be drawn. After that, the beetle can be drawn in any order and throws of the dice entitle players to add on the following:

    4 for a leg
    3 for an antenna
    2 for an eye
    1 for the mouth

As soon as a beetle is completed, either player shouts 'beetle!' – which is the signal for everyone else in the room to stop play immediately and tot up their own score. Legs are the hardest to get, six throws of four being needed.

Winning pairs move forward a table, losing ones move back a table for the next stage of the beetle drive, with play continuing until one or two rounds have been completed, the pair with the highest score each winning a prize.

A booby prize is usually awarded for the lowest score –

A completed beetle!

and, perhaps, an extra joker's prize for the best-drawn or
worst-drawn beetle as a surprise ending to the festivities.

Don't forget to allow for the cost of prizes for winners.

Variations on a theme

WHIST DRIVES are still as popular as ever. Allocate each pair
of partners a small quantity of paper flags, with a flag to be
forfeited or gained when each game is won or lost. Much
easier to keep check on scores this way, and lots more fun
than adding up sums!

TREASURE HUNT

A treasure hunt can either be of the miniature variety, using
a duplicated map for each entrant to mark the treasure trail
leading to a place where they think the treasure trove has
been hidden. Or, if your group feels a little more adventurous,
there are plenty of possibilities for real-life treasure hunting
outdoors. A large garden, recreation ground, park, housing
estate . . . treasure really can be found anywhere, just as long
as you can arrange for some unobtrusive observer to make
sure that it does not fall into the wrong hands!

But, whether your treasure-hunting is done from a cosy

chair or out in the wilds, you must have a good set of clues, each one leading on to the next part of the treasure trail.

These can be written in rhyme, prose or represented by some sort of sign – anything you like. With just a little imagination, a fairly brief examination of a map will provide inspiration for the first step of the treasure trail. For example, the name of a street, well-known store or landmark:

> 'Take the 'st' from 'Highest tree'
> Split them up – remove the 'e'.
> Put 'S' at the tree-top, and 't' down below –
> And you'll find a place that you surely will know – no. 73!'

Answer: 73 High Street!

Or – more easily – ♔ and ⚓ becomes THE CROWN AND ANCHOR!

And once the start has been decided you should generally find that the rest of the clues and stages in your treasure hunt follow quite naturally.

Motor rally enthusiasts are often quite adept at looking at maps and working out clues. Remember too, to stipulate that no clues must be destroyed, spoiled or misplaced along the way, otherwise the competitor is automatically disqualified.

Charge an entrance fee for each competitor to cover profit over and above the cost of prizes (or value for donated items) – three or four prizes for the first treasure hunters to complete the course, plus a dozen or so packets of sweeties and toiletries to console the late arrivals along the way. Plus, of course, any advertising costs, pencils and paper for the contestants, etc. if needed.

And all this is little more than the cost of an ordinary raffle.

THE PRICE IS RIGHT

This is another of those ideas adapted from a popular television show, though on a much smaller scale. Instead of holidays abroad and video equipment, your group should provide prizes such as a box of groceries, a gift voucher, chocolates or home-baked cakes – whatever prizes you may be given.

However, the idea is basically the same – for competitors

to guess the price or combined prices of whatever prizes are on offer. Take them from one source only – i.e. a particular supermarket or department store.

Bear in mind that a fund-raising event should involve everyone who pays money to attend. Avoid confining the fun to small teams near the start of the proceedings. Change the rules of the game just slightly, and have three or four eliminating rounds, with everyone in the audience trying to guess the correct price for – say – half a dozen items, such as a box of eggs, packet of soap, tin of talc, baby doll, pair of tights and a packet of plasters, writing their answers on previously-distributed slips of paper.

Give ten points for a fully correct answer, and five points for a near miss – these marks are announced to the audience by a master of ceremonies, together with all the correct prices. Competitors estimating higher than the correct price are 'busted', but anyone claiming correct or 'just below' answers is invited to stand or hold up their slip of paper for verification by helpers or fellow members of the audience. Allow a good few minutes at this stage for some lively discussion!

Everyone then calculates their final score and those with the highest number of points compete for the main prize.

These top-scorers play the next round of the game on the stage, writing each estimate of the price of an item on a large sheet of cardboard or paper, so that these may be seen by the audience. They are announced in turn by the master of ceremonies, using the target of a total cost score, rather than a points system, as a change from the first part of the programme, i.e. –

Box of chocolates £5
Packet of cigars £7
Bottle of perfume £10
                                    TOTAL = £22

and this £22 is the target score. So the competitor scoring an overall cost nearest to this total is the winner. The second nearest wins the runner-up prize, and so on.

For a little added interest, and to keep the audience occupied, all those not on stage can also write down their estimated prices, with the person scoring nearest the overall cost winning a consolation prize.

Around a dozen prizes, large and small, should be enough for one evening's entertainment – and this should give you some idea of the profit-making potential for this particular idea.

FASHION SHOWS

Although most fund-raising fashion shows are aimed at the ladies, men's fashions should be featured as well, particularly now that gentlemen's clothes are constantly becoming more colourful and imaginative.

The basic ingredients are a hall – one with a stage, if possible. Otherwise, try to arrange seating with a central aisle. And you need either a department store, or ladies' boutique and/or men's outfitters, who are willing to promote their own merchandise for a good cause. Make a few enquiries at your favourite shops, or flip through the local paper to see who is spending most on advertising, and you are sure to hit on a winner, once you put the idea of a fashion show into their head!

It's up to the shop to supply all the clothes, models and whatever background music they prefer. If you want your fashion show to be the first in a long line of successful events, be as helpful as you can, especially if you happen to know a cheap-and-cheerful disc jockey. Local hospital radio is always a good possibility, in return for a mention on the programme, and a donation towards hospital funds – all in a good cause!

Remember too, to choose a venue which has enough space for clothes and for models to change behind the scenes. There should be mirrors and running water fairly close at hand.

Prepare programmes for your audience so that they can note any outfits which take their fancy. Make an admission charge, to include refreshments. Most stores will agree to a 5% or 10% commission for you on goods ordered at the show, which makes extra promotion very worthwhile!

WEDDING EXHIBITION

Weddings are big business for many traders: photographers, caterers, dressmakers, dress hire shops, jewellers, outfitters, video makers, florists . . .

You can get them all together for a wedding exhibition

which will interest prospective brides, and their families. The main requirement is a good venue, preferably one which is used for wedding receptions.

Look in the local press or Yellow Pages for addresses and telephone numbers to try. Choose a suitable date for your exhibition and negotiate a reasonable hire fee.

Your team can then approach the various business concerns to interest them in exhibiting. And if you divide the cost of two extra exhibitors between those attending, you will find that the extra income will pay for background music and a disc jockey to compère a mini fashion show of wedding dresses and accessories.

Your profit will come from the entrance charges made to prospective brides and their families, ploughmen's lunches and refreshments, and exhibitors' fees, plus commission from the exhibitors on new business gained through the exhibition, with a possible added bonus by way of introductory commission on advertising space sold to exhibitors for a special feature by the local paper, with some free publicity for your fund-raising group.

SQUARE DANCES (or 'HOE-DOWNS')
Just in case you aren't too sure about it, square dancing is a form of dancing within a square formation of eight couples, the 'square' always beginning and ending each dance 'set'.

It's easy to learn, even for people who have never quite managed any other sort of dancing before. Everyone changes partners a number of times during the course of each dance, so the square-dancers soon begin talking and enjoying themselves together. An instant cure for shyness and one of the easiest ways to make new friends!

The most important 'basic requirement' of square dancing is the 'caller', whose job it is to call instructions in time to the foot-tapping music. He supplies the music and all necessary equipment. You need only provide an electric socket and a place to dance in. So, as well as the hire charge for a hall, set aside the caller's fee and any expenses in preliminary costings.

For further details and how to get a list of callers operating in your area, please refer to appendix (7) (page 124).

PARTY NIGHT

Party night is meant to be a good old-fashioned family occasion, characterised by the complete absence of modern-day trappings such as disco lights, recorded music, microphones etc.

Choose instead such innocent pleasures as musical chairs, pass-the-parcel, postman's knock, blind man's buff, hunt the thimble and all the other favourite parlour games which your group will remember with delight. Other highlights should be a hearty sing-song around the piano, the hokey-cokey, parlour ballads, comic monologues, a talent spot, and all the other trimmings of a family party which it seems many children these days sadly have yet to enjoy.

Invite each of your committee members to contribute one item towards a planned, or semi-planned programme and keep all guests, young and old, happily amused, whatever the scale of the occasion.

MUSICAL EVENING

A fund-raising musical evening is an alternative to a party night. The main difference is that guests and fund-raisers contribute items in the form of a concert programme, with fellow guests enjoying the performance mainly as an audience, rather than taking an active part.

Here is an extra fund-raising factor pointed out to me by a very shrewd businessman employed in the field of showbiz entertainment. If you manage to enlist the help of a good amateur orchestra or choir this then widens the appeal for tickets, which are likely to be bought by friends and relatives of the performers!

Design a programme which can be sold at the musical evening, along with refreshments at the interval – plus door money of course. All proceeds to your favourite cause!

MASKED BALL

Everyone's idea of a dance with a difference, one which can be adapted for an informal disco party as well as a dinner dance.

The fun and enjoyment of a masked ball centres on a delicious sense of secrecy – i.e. who is wearing which mask? True, a particular person's height, build, gait and the clothes they may be wearing can give the game away. But there are always some surprises during the course of the evening, leading up to the 'de-masking ceremony', where small prizes may also be awarded for the best mask, judged by an appointed panel or volume of applause from the other guests.

The de-masking ceremony should also consist of a guessing game for everyone to join in, trying to state each masked person's identity (partners excluded) with a prize for any 'Missed-Guest/Mis-Guessed' who cannot be correctly challenged and identified.

For an extra dash of originality, you could always introduce a ten point challenge, with everyone bringing a note-book or being issued with a postcard on arrival. Then, at an appropriate part of the proceedings, each table takes it in turns to try and challenge as many other masked guests on other tables as possible, within a time limit. Eager voices are liable to give other masked guests plenty of clues here!

Or – if you are reasonably sure that everyone can stand the pace – you will find that a free-for-all challenge (with all tables taking part at the same time, and no 'taking turns') is rather more exciting, although five times as hectic!

INDOOR GAMES TOURNAMENTS
Another very flexible idea which any group could arrange. It can be a one day 'knock-out' tournament, starting off with – for example – 100 players, each needing to win three clear games to be among the 50 players going through to the next round.

50 players will then, of course, result in an odd number of 25 winners, ready to play the next round. But whenever you come up against the odd number problem, you can always introduce a wild card, where the names of all losing competitors get put into a hat and the winner of this 'lucky dip' takes the wild card to get back into the contest. This gives a reason for people to stay and enjoy the tournament, if there is a chance of getting back into the prize-winning stakes!

Which game to play? Well, although games such as chess and cribbage may immediately spring to mind, not everyone can play them – and fund-raisers need to attract as many people as possible. So choose a game, or games, which more people are likely to have at home. Dominoes, tiddledywinks and draughts are all strong contenders.

Or, to give the most inexperienced player a good chance of winning a prize, you might plump for a games medley of snakes and ladders, ludo (bearing in mind that both these games can be played by *two* people, as would be the case in a games tournament, rather than the full quota of four players) or even hang-man, where the first player writes down a dash to represent each letter of a famous person's name (can be a television celebrity, film star, etc. as specified). The second player then tries to guess which letters comprise the name, by saying letters one at a time. Correctly-guessed letters are entered in their appropriate places, but for each letter incorrectly guessed, a line is drawn as part of a hanged man (you can have a maximum of 12 guesses).

For example, in the following game the 'guesser' has guessed 6 letters of this film star's/famous celebrity's name – B O B _ O P E – in 5 guesses because the one correct guess 'O' is entered twice, in the christian and surname. But there were also 11 incorrect letters guessed at, with one piece of the hang-man for each one, as shown below.

If the guessing competitor does not correctly guess the letter 'H' to begin this famous man's surname, then the final cross-

stroke is drawn (see above) and the first player wins this game. Vice versa if the guesser correctly guesses the letter 'H'.

'Hang-man' is just about the most widely played and popular of all school games, so if you do not remember playing it, enlist the help of your children in re-learning the rules! These 'golden oldies' are always fun.

Or you could set up an indoor games club, with matches each week at different people's houses. In remote areas, with an indoor games group, either telephone or post weekly results to a group secretary organising a league table on much the same way as soccer clubs, with bonus points awarded for the highest score. In this case, you could also introduce more time-consuming games such as Scrabble, Monopoly or Cluedo for extra interest, with perhaps just one or two games played per match, according to what members prefer.

Work out the charges for weekly subscriptions for an indoor games group, or the price of a ticket for a one-day tournament, where you could also set up a few other attractions, such as pick-a-dish (see page 81) and tombola (see page 53) to attract funds from well-wishers and onlookers enjoying the occasion at a modest admission charge.

Variations on a theme
PRIZE BINGO is still as popular as it ever was, especially among regular players. No cash prizes are offered to players and

children can join in the fun.

DARTS TOURNAMENTS always attract attention, both from regular players and would-be champions (you could well be surprised by one or two big names coming along to take part). Supporters can come along and watch and boost the takings from the bar and ploughmen's lunches or suppers.

For further information on darts tournaments see appendix (8), page 124.

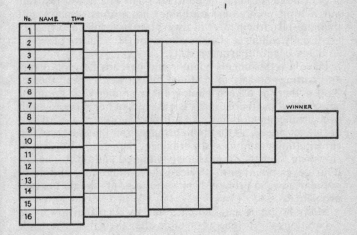

Fig. 9. How to organise a darts tournament for 16 players.

FLOWER FESTIVALS

Flower festivals are regaining the popularity they once had in Victorian and Edwardian times, especially in raising funds for churches and hospitals.

Start off by thinking of a good theme for flower arrangements. One of the most successful which I supported was the theme of 'celebration' to coincide with a church festival to commemorate a most wonderful 850th anniversary. But 'praise', 'gratitude', 'joy', 'prayer', 'love', 'dedication' and 'worship' are just a few other alternatives to set people thinking of ways to express the theme of the festival in flowers.

Invite people to take part by sending in a flower arrange-

ment based on the chosen theme. Begin by contacting all the
floral arrangement clubs (addresses from the public library
or arts department of your local council), voluntary associations, local schools, youth groups and community clubs. Not
everyone can grow flowers or afford to buy them, so you may
like to include classes for wild flowers, handmade paper or
plastic flowers and flower drawings and paintings – always
very popular with children.

No charge is usually made to take part in a flower festival,
but a little programme outlining the various displays and
thanking all participants will always be a fast-seller and visitors
are usually willing to give donations for the pleasure of seeing
so many beautiful arrangements.

Have a refreshments counter and perhaps flowers, plants
and cuttings on sale to continue the 'flower festival' theme.
And if there is a keen photographer among your group of
supporters (and there usually is!) ask him or her to photograph
each arrangement, then make a display of prints to be ordered
at budget prices, so that both arrangers and members of the
contributing group have a permanent memento of the occasion long after the flowers have withered and died. The 24-
hour develop-and-print service is becoming more and more
popular now, so prompt display of the prints should pose no
problem.

Many hospitals and churches like to keep the flowers as
decorations for as long as possible after their flower festival.
But, for extra funds, arrangements can also be sold to the
highest bidder along 'pick-a-dish' lines (see page 81).

CRAFT FAIRS
Hire a decent-sized hall and charge rent for around 25 craft
stalls measuring, on average 6' × 2'. Your group will also
get the admission charges, plus profits from refreshments,
raffles and the proceeds of any stall which you might like to
run yourselves, either crafts or a related topic such as home-
produce, plants or greeting cards.

You can also ask for a 5% or 10% commission on each
stall-holder's takings. That way, you can tell the public that
every penny which they spend helps your good cause.

The main task of planning a craft fair is to track down
enough stall-holders to take part. Visit other fairs and

markets, shops, shows and exhibitions to gather names. Scour local papers. Contact your local authority's arts and entertainments department for addresses of craft groups and workshops. Try not to have more than two or three stall-holders exhibiting the same craft – and make sure that similar ones are well spaced out to give everyone a fair chance.

Once you have your list of names and addresses, hang on to it for dear life! Look after your stall-holders by putting up a plan of the hall and table allocation. Offer them coffee when they arrive. Help them to unpack and set up their stalls. Book them lunch (which they pay for, if not bringing their own sandwiches). Then they will be eager to know when your next craft fair will be and you can start planning it as an annual event which people will look forward to.

Advertising is particularly important for a craft fair, so make sure that you go through the advertising check-lists in Chapter 5, page 35, and see example poster overleaf.

A disappointing turn-out will deter the craftsmen from booking again. But an impressive début will bring them queueing to come next time around, so that you can afford to be choosy and build up a good reputation.

COACH TRIPS

You may not raise a great deal of money from a coach trip but you will make a lot of friends and build up your list of supporters. It does not need a great deal of hard work or lengthy planning.

The easiest way to begin is by announcing the idea under 'any other business' on the committee agenda and say you would like some suggestions of places to visit. There should be attractions to see and to enjoy in rainy weather as well as on fine days. Most leisure parks, zoos and safari parks offer generous reductions for party bookings.

Then check coach hire firms in the Yellow Pages and ask for quotations for various size coaches to go to your chosen venue.

Divide the all-inclusive figure by the number of seats to get the cost price per person. Add 15% for each person for profit. Your fellow travellers still save themselves money and the coach trip works out very nicely as a fund-raising day out for helpers and supporters too!

Fig. 10. Example Poster for a Craft Fair.

PRAM RACE

Some national charities have pram-racing off to a fine art and other fund-raisers can make the same idea work.

Get as many old prams as possible – not generally a problem. A team for each pram consists of at least two 'nannies' prepared to push a 'baby' in the pram. Teams can be from shops, department stores, offices, factories, youth clubs, in fact any source the organisers care to approach.

Next thing the organisers must do is to decide a place for the *end* of the race and list all the pubs within a mile and a half to a two-mile radius. Almost certainly, there will be far more than anyone realises!

On pram race day, the competitors assemble at an agreed starting point, with each team having to visit at least twelve pubs and collect witnesses' signatures as proof, before racing ahead to the finishing line.

Many pram race committees also require that at least one member of each team should have a drink in every pub they visit, so as to make certain that the pubs do get extra business. But this is not strictly necessary as people always seem anxious to follow peculiar-looking nannies and babies right up to the bar if need be!

Needless to say, all babies and nannies carry collecting tins ready for amused passers-by and pub customers to dig into their pockets.

Further profits come from sponsor deals from supporters of each team for the number of pubs visited or the final position in the race.

Award prizes for the winning team, the team collecting the highest amount and the best decorated pram, and remember to advise/consult your local police in good time of the date of your pram race in case there are any bye-laws which apply.

RACE NIGHT

I know that many fund-raising committees cannot countenance any form of gambling so I am reluctant to outline betting procedures for this particular idea, although the money-making potential for 'race night' from a gambler's point of view will soon become obvious.

A race consists of six riders and six runners. The rider sits on a chair, back towards the runner or horse, so that no rider

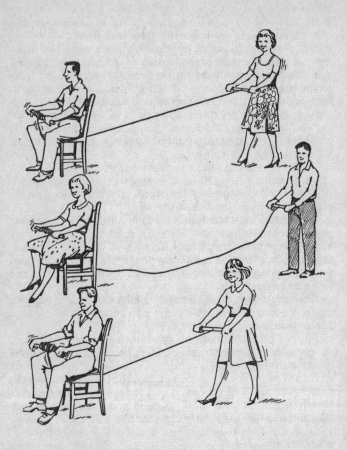

Fig. 11. Race Night.
'Riders' sit on chairs with their backs to 'runners'. Each rider winds a length of string, which leads from under their chair, around a piece of wood. The other ends of the strings are held by the runners. As the riders wind the strings (as fast as they can) the runners move forward. Runners must not move until tugged by the winding-on of the strings!

may see which horse is moving the fastest. A horse may *only* move when tugged forward by a long length of string which goes under the rider's chair, with the rider then winding the string around a spindle or piece of wood just as fast as he or she can. All the spindles or pieces of wood must be the same size. The winner is the first to reach the chair.

The spectators begin to see the horses edging forward, being pulled by their string and they will cheer the runners on, just as in a real horse race!

Variations on a theme
DONKEY DERBYS always attract a lot of interest, mainly because of the unpredictable nature of donkeys . . . Six or eight donkeys are all you need, giving them different names and pedigrees for each race.

MUSIC HALL
If you yearn for a successful fund-raising occasion which people will talk about and remember for months afterwards, a music hall will fit the bill admirably! The unpretentious atmosphere, the exhortations to 'join in with the singing', and the amateurish acts add to the flavour of this unique style of entertainment. 'Second-raters' nobly suffer boos and cat-calls at the bottom of the bill!

If your group has a music hall enthusiast willing to take complete charge of the proceedings, all well and good. Otherwise, simply follow the example of enterprising pub landlords in Victorian and Edwardian times and compile your own bill of artistes ready to entertain your audience. Most important of all, have a good pianist to provide versatile accompaniment throughout the evening and an entertaining master of ceremonies to keep the audience in order and announce the various acts.

Try the 'anyone brave enough' acts which have always been a feature of music hall; you could well find yourself being beseiged by supporters and members of your own group wanting to 'tread the boards' with a few monologues or comic songs.

Although amateur acts do not charge for their performances, it is usual to meet their expenses – normally kept to a minimum for fund-raising causes. The pianist, being the most hard-working of all, deserves something. You may be lucky enough to discover your own master of ceremonies among your supporters. But, unless you know him very well, the offer of expenses is always very much appreciated and generally means that he will be more likely to oblige your group on a future occasion.

Another authentic feature of the music hall is that the bar should be kept going continually through the evening. Each group of people at a table writes their order on a slip of paper and holds this up for a barmaid to collect and write the amount due at the bottom of the paper, ready for payment when the drinks are delivered at the table. Barmaids are participants for whom Victorian dress is an absolute 'must'. A plain black dress or long black skirt with a black blouse, frilly cap and a white apron will do.

There are also many light operatic groups who provide a complete Victorian music hall presentation, along with pianist and master of ceremonies. Contact your local arts and entertainments offices for the names and addresses of any groups near you and enquire what their fees are.

Variation on a theme

A PIERROT or END-OF-THE-PIER SHOW is on a slightly smaller scale than the music hall, and held in a garden or school playground, with sea-side refreshments such as ice-creams, lollies, fizzy drinks, candy floss, shellfish and fruit squashes in place of a bar.

Ice-cream van men are usually pleased to come along and do some extra business, providing a percentage of the profit towards your funds.

And don't forget to have a sea-side sing-song!

DISCO DANCES

The great attraction about disco dances is that they are so easy to arrange. Just take one hall, one disc jockey, a collection of records, lights and jokey remarks and the fund-raising is done.

Or so people imagine. Until they try to sell tickets and detect a lack of enthusiasm at the prospect of dancing all evening to an endless stream of recorded music, much like hundreds of other disco dances they've been to and haven't enjoyed particularly.

So try and introduce some sort of novelty ingredient here.

A fancy dress disco, a ragamuffins' disco dance, a desert island disco dance or a hilly-billy discomania – all with suitable (optional) costumes, decorations, prizes and a few party games such as musical chairs and pass-the-parcel to keep the fun going.

Variations on a theme

SUPPER DANCES – any dance or party with a special break for a fish-and-chip supper, pizza or hot potato specials. Many fish-and-chip shops and take-away restaurants will give you a quotation for a party service. Add this to the hire of your hall, charge for a disc jockey and printing of tickets and add your profit on the basis of realistic numbers.

SUPER SPONSORS

Ordinary sponsored events tend to be boring, but a little imagination and a sense of fun make all the difference:

matchbox marathon

How many items can you get inside a standard matchbox? Pins, peppercorns, seeds, buttons, needles . . .

One penny per item! Children in the Brownies and Cubs age range really enjoy this type of sponsored event because the practice is just as much fun as the actual count-up. And mums and dads love the challenge of trying to beat each other!

dress-a-dummy

The 'dummy' on this occasion is actually a person – grown-up or child. People taking part form their own teams, each team choosing a 'dummy' who starts off modestly dressed in under-wear and socks. Then at the start of a given time limit – fifteen minutes, for example – each team tries putting as many items of clothing on their dummy as they possibly can, either altogether or one at a time. Sponsor money on a 'per item' basis when the final whistle blows and a lot of fun and giggles watching the dummy being undressed and items being counted at the end of it all.

peanut pushing relay

Silly events like this and its sister race the 'carrot crawl' always attract attention and enjoyment.

Push either a roasted peanut or carrot with your nose along a pre-arranged distance, ready for the next person in the relay to take over. The first peanut-pusher or carrot-crawler races ahead to the next step, ready to take up the race again. It only needs three or four pushers or crawlers to make a team. The winners are the trio or quartet who can complete a lap of a local park in the fastest time, urged on by applauding spectators and sponsors.

Sponsor money can be per inch, foot, yard, metre – or donation per circuit.

quilting party

This idea really originated in the northern states of America, where womenfolk would get together to stitch and sew a patchwork quilt as the first item in a young girl's 'bottom drawer'. And a very practical idea it was too.

The hexagon is the easiest patch to start with and it is always best to draw one on to card (an old cereal packet will do) as a pattern. Using the pattern, cut out seven hexagons from stiff brown paper or old greeting cards – ordinary paper is rather too thin and flimsy. And do not cut more than two hexagons at a time, otherwise they will all be slightly different sizes.

The material you use can be from old clothes in the ragbag, scraps of fabric or remnant pieces. If there's a clothing factory nearby, they may well let you have some offcuts for nothing. Cotton is the perfect fabric to use, because it is cheap, hardwearing and there should be lots of patterns and colours to mix and match in your patchwork.

Fig. 12. Patchwork Quilting.

1. Place paper hexagon on 'wrong side' of larger fabric hexagon.
2. Fold edges of fabric hexagon over paper hexagon.
3. Tack all round, through both paper and fabric.
4. 'Right sides' facing, stitch one side of two patches together, taking care not to sew through paper hexagons.
5. Remove a paper hexagon when all sides of a patch have been stitched or oversewn.
6. A 'patchwork flower'. Join lots of patches together to make a larger item, e.g. a bedspread.

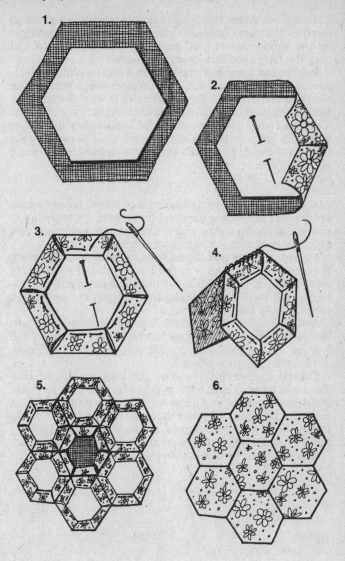

Trim fabric pieces into rough hexagon shapes, large enough to cover the paper hexagons comfortably. Lay one hexagon on the wrong side of each piece, pin into place, then fold over the fabric and tack on to the paper.

Patches can then be stitched together with an ordinary over-sewing or buttonhole stitch. Join together seven hexagons of the same material to make a 'patchwork flower'. Join all your patches together in a random style or using patchwork flowers. You can collect sponsor money for the number of patches sewn and you will also have a splendid quilt to use for your own good cause, as a raffle prize or as a donation to some deserving charity.

sing-song

Although a sponsored sing-song may consist of the same song or group of songs sung over and over again, it's more fun to provide a good medley which most people can enjoy and maybe join in with a well-known chorus.

Everyone taking part should write down all the songs which they can sing by heart – and there are bound to be many more than you might think! Writing them down and remembering half-forgotten melodies, from nursery rhymes to love songs, is only half the fun!

Make enough copies of all the lists for everyone taking part before you select a venue for your sing-song. Almost any hall will do, as long as you have made sure of enough publicity. A first-class pianist is needed.

On the day, work through all the songs on all the lists. Take it in turns to have a ten minute rest each hour or three-quarters of an hour and invite all visitors to join in with the melodies and choruses whilst they stay to have some refreshments, buy a few home-bakes, try their luck on a raffle or tombola and sponsor the group at so much per song.

The whole event should turn into quite a party!

9

GOING INTO BUSINESS

Nowadays there are more fund-raising business opportunities than ever before – mail order catalogues, shopping clubs, gift parties, 'charity' shops etc. New schemes seem to be forever on the increase, each offering yet another method of acquiring a regular source of income, plus a way of attracting a wide range of new supporters.

On the whole, such fund-raising can work out very well. There is no panic about collecting goods to display and sell by a certain time. Prices tend to be much higher than at one-day fund-raising events where buyers can sometimes strike a very hard bargain. And no unpacking and no packing-up to do when the last customer has gone home!

If your group is considering a business enterprise, then be sure to have enough supporters to keep everything running smoothly. About 10–15 people for running a charity shop is the absolute minimum. Remember that not all volunteers can work a regular day each week. As well as sales, you will need to cope with cleaning, display, accounting and publicity – all of which will need staff.

In a voluntary organisation it is best to have at least two joint managers in charge of the shop so that one or the other is always there and rotas, stock, sales and paper work can be properly co-ordinated.

Premises are generally easy to obtain. Most boroughs and local authorities have an arrangement whereby empty shops owned by them can be taken over by non profit-making concerns until the shop is leased to a new tenant.

For example, if you see empty shop premises at ground level of a council-built precinct or housing estate, then those premises are probably council-owned and you can make enquiries through the leasing or lettings department of the local authority. Neighbouring shops will be able to give you the appropriate name and address if you enquire and it is also worth contacting the local authority if you see an empty shop with no information or estate agent's hoarding on display.

Once you have found your shop the only expenses which usually have to be met are such items as gas and electricity. The majority of local authorities take the view that they would rather have a responsible tenant fund-raising for a good cause in their premises than have the shop remain empty over a long period with the risk of damage and vandalism. Therefore, no rent or rates are generally charged, although this is likely to vary from one local authority to another.

Sometimes it may be possible to rent an empty shop privately on a short-term basis, normally through an estate agent and in such cases, fund-raising groups can apply for a reduction in rates, subject to the discretion of the local authority.

This type of letting is only made on the strict understanding that the premises will be promptly vacated by the fund-raising group once a permanent tenant wishes to take over the lease and move in. This can mean that the group has only a matter of days to pack up and get out, but most fund-raisers consider that this inconvenience is outweighed by the opportunity to make extra money, plus the chance to progress from a temporary to a permanent occupancy once the shopkeeping business has become established.

Once you have signed a short-term agreement for your shop, allow at least ten days before opening. It will need a good clean-up. The time will also enable the group to draw up a supply of posters, announcements and news items for the local papers.

Publicise some special 'opening day' bargain offers, such as 'half prices before 12 noon' or 'two items for the price of one'. Most callers to charity shops tend to become regular customers and you will find that it pays to spoil them in the early stages!

Surprisingly, there is no problem collecting enough stock to sell, providing this is controlled. Give all your supporters as much advance notice as possible that you are opening a shop and would welcome any saleable donations, large or small. Get the same message across to people who are moving house (or, better still, emigrating!) as well as those in church-based groups, schools, clubs and businesses.

Once your shop is actually open, you will get donations

and you can always put posters in the windows or on display inside the shop for any specific class of item which you may require.

All charity shops have to conform with health and safety regulations. Under the Office, Shops and Railway Premises Act 1963, you have to register your shop with your local authority and abide by all rulings on lighting, fire precautions, washing facilities, provision of first aid equipment etc. These are also laid down by the Health and Safety at Work Act 1974, along with guidelines for the safety and well-being of members of the public on the premises.

Ask the crime prevention officer based at your nearest police station to advise you on security, free-of-charge. Get all the advice you possibly can on the vexed subject of shop-lifting and the type of till or cash register you should be using. You could hire or buy second-hand equipment. If this makes it doubly difficult for a thief to grab a handful of cash whilst customers are being served, then it is obviously money well spent.

Enquire whether any business proprietors among your supporters would be willing to lend or donate an old cash register which has been superseded.

Appeal for shop-fittings, dress rails, dummy-models, shelving or display cabinets but remember to keep the shop as clutter-free as possible. It annoys people if there are too many things on display, leaving little space to move around comfortably and find what they want.

Pay particular attention to the window because this is the first impression which customers will get of your shop. It is best to display just a few quality items in good condition, rather than a whole range of tired-looking ornaments and out-of-date clothes. Change the window display as often as you like – the more the better.

If your group does not have sufficient funds to renew chipped or peeling paintwork, then at least make sure it is clean and well-scrubbed, perhaps with some coloured lights or bunting to cheer things up and catch the eye.

BE BUSINESSLIKE

Keep a note of everything you spend, right from the start. After all, a shop is a business, even without paid staff or

V.A.T. payable on goods sold. Maintain a total record of sales and expenses so that the managers can keep track of what profits are being made.

Adopt a simple pricing system which both staff and customers will find easy to follow, especially where clothes are concerned.

No price labels leave staff open to hard bargaining from customers, which in the end, defeats the purpose of the shop. Individual price tabs or tickets may be impractical, but it is no hardship to arrange items on one rail or one shelf all costing the same price and keeping the various sections – e.g. children's clothes, women's fashions, paperback books, household goods, etc. – well defined, like separate departments in a store.

List each item you sell and the price charged, especially in the early stages of business, so that you can see the main source of your income. Then, if you find yourself overstocked with one type of merchandise, that is the time to advertise a 'bargain basement dress sale' or 'bedtime book bonanza', both to even out your stock and to attract additional custom. Move fast and keep interest alive!

OTHER BUSINESS IDEAS

Of course, not all fund-raising groups can run a shop. But do not rule out business ventures altogether.

There are a number of fund-raising gift catalogues freely available, offering wide-ranging selections of gift wrappings, greeting cards, gifts and novelties. Fund-raisers distribute these among friends and neighbours, collecting orders on a commission or discount basis, with all profits going to the cause. Remember however, that gift catalogues aren't printed and posted to fund-raisers out of the kindness of the company's heart! The company exists to make money for itself too.

The maximum 20–25% discount offered by the average mail order gift catalogue can usually be up-graded to a 30% or even 40% profit margin by going directly to a wholesaler, most of whom are pleased to accept new business from fund-raising groups.

Such wholesalers issue their own catalogues and special promotions leaflets throughout the year, offering goods at special wholesale prices. Some goods, such as greeting cards, small 'pocket money' toys and Christmas items, are not sold singly but only in 'packs'. So, if one customer wants to buy a giant-size greeting card, two other purchasers may need to be found before the pack of three cards can be bought at a wholesale price. Larger items such as Christmas trees, play equipment, bicycles, large toys, musical cards and wedding novelties are usually sold singly. For the more expensive items it may pay to ask for a deposit.

Delivery can usually be arranged, but will probably be charged for. Alternatively, you could gain an additional 'non packing' and/or collection discount if you collect directly from the wholesaler on a 'cash-and-carry' basis, with the additional benefit of seeing just what is in stock, plus the promotions and special offers on display from which your group may be able to make more money.

Start by visiting local confectioner/tobacconist/newsagent, stationery, greeting card and toy wholesalers in your area. Get their names from Yellow Pages, local chamber of trade and commerce, or simply ask friends and supporters employed in local stores who their wholesalers are and pay them a call.

10

BECOMING A REGISTERED CHARITY

Most fund-raising groups have been established for some time before even thinking of becoming a registered charity and this is usually the best course to start with.

So much depends on the target in view. The process of becoming registered as a charity, though reasonably uncomplicated, often takes months rather than weeks. It is therefore impractical for a short-term project such as an old people's party or all-expenses-paid outing for handicapped children.

However, as many of us know, even the most modest enterprises have a habit of blossoming into far more ambitious and permanent schemes. This is when the possibility of proceeding to the status of a registered charity may have some advantage.

Of course, not all fund-raising groups exist for the sole purpose of promoting charitable causes. Raising money for parent teacher associations, political parties, tenants' associations and community groups may all be very worthwhile but nevertheless cannot be classed as charitable.

There are one or two grey areas which call for particular consideration. For instance, an amateur theatrical society needs to raise money in order to stage productions, enter local festivals and replenish stocks of scenery and costumes. But if the society's activities merely promote and fulfil an interest for its own sake, any associated fund-raising group could not be a registered charity.

However, if there were a youth theatre group which met a particular social need and helped foster racial harmony and improved facilities through its activities, this would probably stand a very good chance of achieving charitable status.

The main benefits of becoming a registered charity are financial ones. There is no tax payable on charitable funds earning interest in bank deposit, building society and investment accounts. Charities do not have to pay inheritance tax on bequests and legacies (see appendix (9), page 125).

Most charities are also entitled to special relief from income tax, corporation tax and capital gains tax. Although a registered charity is not exempt from payment of V.A.T., many goods are especially zero rated, particularly those used by handicapped people, or in the course of medical treatment or research. No V.A.T. is payable in respect of non-classified newspaper and magazine advertising for both educational and fund-raising purposes – quite a big money-saver this one!

To obtain further and more specific information, please refer to appendices (9), (10) and (11) on page 125.

Registered charities in the U.K. may also benefit from the latest payroll giving scheme which came into force from April 1987. Under this, supporters of a charity can elect to make donations which are deducted from their pay before tax, thereby getting tax relief up to a maximum of £100 donated in any tax year.

Such a scheme can only be run by an employer and not by individuals and therefore could work very well in respect of business supporters of your fund-raising charity.

Full details are in the leaflet ref. IR65 'Giving to Charity' issued by the Inland Revenue, or Scottish readers may contact The Scottish Council for Community and Voluntary Organisations (see appendix (3), page 122).

House-to-house appeals, flag-days, street collections and permanently-based collecting boxes or tins are all further fund-raising possibilities, assuming that a charity has enough helpers, once the appropriate licence has been granted according to regulations imposed by the local authority, details of which can be obtained from a police station.

In the case of public lotteries, a licensing fee is normally charged for non-charitable fund-raising causes, but very often waived in respect of registered charities. For further details regarding tickets, prizes, expenses which may be deducted etc. regarding lotteries and gaming, please refer to appendix (12), page 125.

There may be other benefits to be gained at a local level, such as reduced rent, rates and hire charges on premises used by the charity or special facilities and concessions at council-run workshops and community projects for things like printing and photocopying.

Before any fund-raising group can be considered for registration as a charity there must be what the Charity Commission
for England and Wales calls a 'governing instrument', which
in layman's language simply means a constitution or document
which clearly sets out the group's aims and states clearly the
terms under which the funds are to be administered.

At this stage the committee should appoint a board of
trustees, who are usually the existing officers. They decide
on a draft constitution which can then be drawn up and put
before the rest of the committee for any additions or amend-
ments to be made.

The responsibilities of charity trustees are clearly set out
in leaflet ref. T.P.3 available from the Charity Commission
for England and Wales (see appendix (3), page 121).

The Charity Commission will help, advise and comment
on a draft constitution once the initial application has been
made. In Scotland however, where there is no register of
charities, application must be made in the first instance
directly to the Inland Revenue so that provision may be made
for exemption of tax, see appendix (13), page 125.

Although not strictly necessary, it is usual to employ a
solicitor to finalise the constitution and, unless your group
already enjoys the services of an honorary solicitor, it always
saves time and trouble to consult one who is familiar with
charity law. The Law Society can provide the names and
addresses of such solicitors practising in any given area; for
their address and approximate fee, see appendix (14), page
125.

The group has to submit two copies of the draft constitution,
copies of entries from the minutes book, press cuttings, appeal
leaflets and letters of support – in fact, anything which substan-
tiates and provides information about the activities of the
group and how it is working to achieve its aims – along with
copies of any accounts going back three years.

Then, if the draft constitution is agreed in principle by the
appropriate registration body, the final trust deed is drawn
up as a legally-binding document. It incorporates any alterations and additional recommendations made by the Charity
Commission or Inland Revenue and this applies particularly
to the administration of funds in the event of a charity failing

to reach its proposed target or ceasing to function.

The trust deed then becomes the 'governing instrument' – i.e. the 'rules' by which the charity functions and which the trustees must adhere to. For example, unless there is provision in the constitution for the trustees to propose some change of purpose in the work of the charity, then they cannot make such changes without consulting first with the Charity Commission or Inland Revenue and applying to make the necessary alterations in the trust deed.

Similarly, the trustees have no power to alter procedures in management and administration of funds, except as provided for in the constitution.

All of this illustrates:

(a) why becoming a registered charity can often take longer than is expected, and
(b) the wisdom of employing a solicitor who is well versed in charity matters!

A registered charity must notify the Charity Commissioners if it *wants* to make any change in its trust deed – it cannot *make* the change and *then* notify. And, if there is no provision in the constitution for such changes to be made, then the Charity Commission must advise on whether or not the constitution itself can be altered and placed on record in its amended state.

Registered charities are required to keep annual statements of account on record for at least seven years and they must also send statements to the Charity Commission or Inland Revenue on request. A free leaflet 'Charity Accounts' is available from the Charity Commission for England and Wales (see appendix (3), page 121).

The Commission also operates The Charities Official Investment Fund, in which any charity may invest. This operates in much the same way as a unit trust fund, offering a wide range of investments, plus expert investment management which smaller charities in particular would be unable to afford. Further information – from the Charity Commission (page 121).

But of all the many benefits and advantages of becoming a registered charity, perhaps the most important is the protection of funds.

Not only are people likely to give more generously to a named charity, but a charity has the right, through its elected trustees, to state precisely how funds are to be used, with advice and guidance on hand from the Charity Commission.

As one fund-raiser explained: "As a smallish fund-raising group, our committee did sometimes worry whether the money we made might in the future be spent in a way in which we had not intended, should anything happen to prevent the group from functioning, or if a new committee were voted in with different aims to ours.

But becoming a registered charity, with a trust deed on record, it is our insurance policy, if you like, for peace of mind, and to know that the work which we began can continue for its original purpose, until such time good reason is shown for changes to be made, but always with the interests of the charity very much at heart."

11

KEEP UP THE GOOD WORK

Fund-raising is a constantly challenging business. Reach one target and another is staring you in the face, whether this happens to be the cost of converting a recently acquired building, equipping a hostel or raising money for the next much-needed amenity at a school or play-group ...

But take heart. Things *do* get easier once people can see positive proof of your efforts and especially if they can respond with some practical offers of help – such as wall-papering, pouring out teas or taking part in some kind of renovation programme.

So make sure that as many people as possible have the opportunity to celebrate your good news and to share in the satisfaction as well as the rewards for all your hard work.

Publicly announce your group's achievements in as many ways as you can think of, through press, radio and local television programmes as well as contacting those groups and individuals who have supported your organisation. Invite them along to your special 'hand-over' presentation.

This might take the form of a 'magic key' which opens a box or chest containing ignition keys to a mini-bus, or a written guarantee for newly-purchased equipment, or a simple declaration of ownership or achievement on a commemorative scroll or plaque recording the proceedings.

Or commemorate your success with the planting of a tree or small rose garden, a dinner dance, a 'first person to ...' or 'first user of ...' ceremony, or a specially conducted tour.

By creating a unique occasion, you and your colleagues could invite some news-worthy person to come along and mastermind cutting a tape or opening a door. Even if you miss out on a celebrity, you should get a letter or message of congratulation which provides another focus for publicity.

Try too, to arrange an open day for the general public. This may appear strange if it applies to a project such as acquiring an old people's mini-bus or wheel-chair for a disabled athlete – but let some imaginative people decorate that same mini-bus with streamers and balloons and drive around with a group of sing-songing senior citizens to delight many appreciative audiences. Or stage a special celebratory match or sports meeting.

Look out for attractions which may be right on your doorstep!

"We have a simply beautiful queen and two charming princesses, complete with all their regalia," the chairman of a local carnival committee reminded me not so long ago. "It seems such a shame that so few people bother about asking them to put in an appearance at a special event, especially when the press is always so keen to photograph them and report on what they are doing . . ."

Check whether the interest in your activities and achievement extends to those who would derive positive benefit from the results of your hard work.

Make an effort to involve the families and friends of these people in your future programme, by inviting them to social occasions such as coffee mornings, afternoon teas and whist drives – always remembering that some people never like going *anywhere* without a personal invitation.

Make a stir about new schemes to finance additions to the original target as well.

A trampoline in a play-area to celebrate the birth of a grandchild – a garden seat outside a senior citizens' day centre to commemorate a silver or golden wedding anniversary – a bird bath in the grounds of a hospital in memory of a loved one – all practical, useful ways of encouraging people outside your fund-raising circle to make a positive and lasting contribution to your cause.

Giving is just as important as receiving! A local drama or musical festival may seem to have little connection with the object of your fund-raising, but can provide a valuable opportunity to reach out and extend both the name and the activities of your group into completely new areas. People who may have no knowledge of or inclination towards your objectives get to learn more and to develop real interest.

For instance, some of the very best amateur theatre in the country can be seen in a drama festival of one-act plays near my home each year. The main trophy is accompanied by a cheque for only £15, donated by a local paper, yet the modesty of this award detracts neither from the high standard of the presentations nor from the keen competitive spirit of the festival.

Each year, the local paper is widely publicised for the sake of a £15 prize and it attracts interest and increased circulation from all the drama festival participants, their families and friends, the audiences, adjudicators and theatre staff. And the third prize in this same festival is £5 ...

A trophy returned each year need only cost a matter of pounds, which even when accompanied by a cash prize, is still an affordable amount, probably less than a small advertisement in your local paper. It would be an on-going reminder of your cause and a regular focal point for renewed interest and commemoration. Could you link the timing of the award with a special event for your group, for example, the date of your public appeal or the day when the target was finally reached?

In fact *all* memorable days are worth being recorded by celebrations and fund-raising events, especially with competitions and fun attractions in which any member of the public can take part.

One group I know equipped a complete under-sixteen youth football team and reserves with T-shirts suitably emblazoned on the back with their name and emblem, in return for a weekly mention and/or news paragraph in the programme for both home and away matches.

This was extremely successful in making the organisation known to a completely new audience; it was also found that donations from the parents and relatives of the team members, collections amongst spectators and special fund-raising by the boys themselves, more than covered the total outlay on the T-shirts. The football team also gained lots of new supporters through their efforts in helping with the fund-raising.

Approach your local arts and entertainments officer, or ask the advice of the regional arts council if your group is stuck for some ideas. Any offers of help and opportunities to foster new interest will surely be welcome!

How do you judge your success? Well – when you see a total stranger smiling happily as he or she walks away from any event which you have organised, feeling satisfied at having had an enjoyable time – as well as from helping a worthy cause – who then begins looking forward to the next occasion – there is no more for you to learn about *fund-raising without fail.*

12

MONEY WELL SPENT

Targets have been reached. Your fund-raising group is flourishing, and if the cash situation isn't exactly sparkling, at least money is coming in at a steady pace.

So, what do you spend it on? One thing's for certain – there will never be any shortage of suggestions! But, as with any other matter of finance or investment, the main consideration must always be *value* for money.

Specially-adapted equipment for one hostel inmate may be desperately needed. But, is there any way in which the cost could be shared with another, similarly handicapped person? Could the same amount of money be spent to benefit a greater number of equally deserving patients?

Alternatively, is the cost of the equipment needed likely to increase to such an extent as to put a financial strain on resources in the future? Is there a way of monitoring the help given and progress made with the aid of the equipment – help which would assist other patients, or assist in research or a social studies programme?

Although your group may never need to consider such serious and far-reaching decisions as these, everybody will want to see funds being allocated as wisely as possible.

A separate trust committee should be formed as soon as the initial target has been reached, if not before. It should consist not only of members of the fund-raising group, but also representatives of the beneficiaries, as well as one or two people who are able to offer a completely objective view when needed – such as a representative from local industry, company director or bank manager, an individual who is used to dealing with both management and finances at a practical level.

Sometimes, one project has to be relinquished in favour of another, usually when a particularly urgent need is seen against the fast-increasing costs of a major target.

You need to assess whether or not the urgent necessity might be funded through another source, or if a separate fund-raising programme could be launched specifically for that purpose.

But, would this mean shelving the major project and thereby risk a lapse of support? By how much would the target cost for the main project increase if it were shelved for any length of time?

When the solution to any problem seems especially difficult, or if it has all the signs of becoming a long-standing debatable point, the easiest way is often to call an open meeting so that everyone concerned with the project may attend, air their views and offer practical help. People who are involved with a fund-raising group have little or no idea of the difficulties the group may be facing. You may be surprised at the number and variety of suggestions which can spark off new ideas in a frank and open discussion.

The committee as a whole should always ensure that their supporters know about their future aims and what the current target is. One of the most effective ways of doing this is by a regular newsletter to keep everyone informed on social topics, such as engagements, weddings and births, as well as news items about the group and its activities. Newsletters are useful in keeping the local press, radio and civic dignatories fully up-to-date with all that is going on, so they are usually worth the investment and expense of stationery and postage.

Keep an 'open door' for visitors, with frequent occasions such as open evenings and special open committee forums. This way, anyone who is interested may come and watch your committee at work in the course of its normal proceedings, along the same lines as local authority committee meetings. Keep the latter half of the agenda for any confidential matters, when guests and visitors can be politely asked to leave.

Consider setting up a general fund for future investment. Do you need to set aside a sum for unforeseen expenses or emergencies which may arise in the future? This always needs to be considered when the focus of a project has a limited 'life', such as a mini-bus or play equipment. Tax and insurance must be allowed for on vehicles.

The challenge is to keep friends and supporters actively interested in future fund-raising, even though they may prefer to assume that all the hard work is at an end and perhaps not be willing to accept that more is needed to reap the full rewards of past efforts.

So once again, right up to the very end of your project, it is a matter of fund-raising without fail!

People who have looked on your money-making events as occasions on which to meet friends and enjoy themselves would undoubtedly be disappointed if everything stopped suddenly. Consider forming a supporters' club or leisure group, which anyone can subscribe to and join.

However, all good things do eventually come to an end. It is often difficult for dedicated and hard-working fund-raisers to step aside gracefully when someone else is appointed, especially if they also happen to be founder members, in at the very beginning.

Yet views, ideas and approaches need to change, if a group is not to become 'stale'. 'New blood' is essential. Just as a child needs to grow and develop, so do fund-raising groups if they are to survive effectively. You can still carry on helping, and always reflect that no fund-raising programme could ever have started were it not for those long-standing members inspiring others to match their interest and follow their example.

APPENDIX

NOTE: All information and prices quoted are supplied in good faith as being correct at the time of going to press.

1. **FURTHER INFORMATION ON COVENANTS**
From: Inland Revenue, Claims Branch
      St John's House
      Merton Road
      BOOTLE
      Merseyside L69 9BB

2. **THE DIRECTORY OF GRANT-MAKING TRUSTS**
Price for the 1987 edition is quoted as being approximately £48, plus postage and packing, and available from:

    The Charities Aid Foundation
    48 Pembury Road
    TONBRIDGE
    Kent TN9 2LD
    Telephone: Tonbridge (0732) 356323

3. **LOCAL TRUSTS**
The Charity Commission, given the names of up to seven local trusts in England and Wales, will supply further details by post. But where investigation is required as to the existence of local trusts in any particular area, a personal visit is required. Readers in: Cheshire, Cleveland, Cumbria, Derbyshire, Durham, Greater Manchester, Hereford, Humberside, Lancashire, Leicestershire, Lincolnshire, Merseyside, Northumberland, Nottinghamshire, Shropshire, Staffordshire, Tyne & Wear, West Midlands, Worcester, Yorkshire and Wales should contact:

    The Charity Commission
    Northern Office, Graeme House
    Derby Square
    LIVERPOOL L2 7SB
    Telephone: 051-227 3191

Those living in other parts of England should contact:
    The Charity Commission
    Southern Office
    St Alban's House
    57-60 Haymarket
    LONDON SW1Y 4QX
    Telephone: 01-210 4405

A Scottish directory of local trusts is not complete, but a general guide
may be obtained from:
    The Scottish Council for Community and Voluntary
        Organisations
    18/19 Claremont Crescent
    EDINBURGH
    Scotland
    Telephone: 031-556 3882

Also obtainable from this address:
    The Directory of Community Development Organisations
        in Scotland – price £3.50
    Directory of Grant-Making Trusts and Organisations for
        Scotland – price £5.50
    Voluntary Organisations in Scotland – price £4.95

Those readers in Northern Ireland and Eire should contact:
    The Department of Finance and Personnel
    Charities Branch
    Kosepark House
    Upper Newtownard's Road
    BELFAST
    Northern Ireland BT1 3NR

Also available:
    The Foundation Directory (U.S.A.), obtain from
    The Foundation Centre
    79 Fifth Avenue, 16th Street
    New York
    New York State 10003
    U.S.A.
    International Foundation Directory, published by
    European Publications Limited
    18 Bedford Square
    London WC1B 3JN (Price £34, plus postage & packing)

Guide to European Foundations – last published in 1978 by the
Giovanni Agnelli Foundation, it is no longer available for purchase, but
obtainable for on-site reference only at The Charities Aid Foundation,
48 Pembury Road, Tonbridge Kent, as are The Foundation Directory
and International Foundation Directory.

4. RE-CYCLING OF ALUMINIUM CANS FOR FUND-RAISING PURPOSES
Write to: Derek Kemp, Chairman
            The Ali-Can Re-Cycling Scheme
            Atcost Road Barking
            Essex IG11 0EQ

giving the name of the fund-raising cause for which you wish to collect. In return, the scheme will send you, absolutely free (no stamped addressed envelope needed) the Scheme's 'Get You Started' package containing leaflets for collectors, posters to publicise your can-collecting scheme, and thirty special 'Mr Ali-Can Man' plastic sacks, each large enough to hold at least 200 crushed aluminium cans. A presentation video is also available with details of collection arrangements.

5. PLOUGHMEN'S SUPPERS – APPROXIMATE COSTING FOR ONE HUNDRED PEOPLE, including disposable plates, cutlery and napkins to dispense with the chore of washing-up.

10 lettuces, ice-berg variety is by far the best choice for minimum wastage	£8.00
6 – 7 lb tomatoes (½ tomato per plate), price according to season, but say	£5.50
4½ dozen large or medium eggs (½ egg per plate)	£6.75
4 lb Cheddar cheese (cut into chunky fingers)	£5.50
12 French loaves (each cut into ten wedges which are then halved so that each person gets two generous hunks of bread, plus a few pieces over for second helpings)	£5.40
9 dozen disposable plates @ 85p per dozen	£7.65
9 dozen disposable knives & forks @ 85p	£7.65
2 rolls of cling-film	£1.60
2 jumbo packs of paper napkins	£1.60
1 lb butter or low-fat spread	£1.50
	TOTAL: £51.15

Less than 60p per head, even if you spend another pound or two on some jars of pickles and chutney – and the prices quoted are certainly not the lowest cut-prices at the time of going to press either!

6. LICENSED BARS

For a non-licensee to run a licensed bar for fund-raising purposes of any kind, application must be made for OCCASIONAL PERMISSION.

In ENGLAND and WALES the appropriate application form may be obtained from the CLERKS TO THE JUSTICES for the area in which the function is being held.

In SCOTLAND, application must be made to the CLERKS TO THE LICENSING BOARD, under Section 34 of the Licensing in Scotland Act 1976.

Addresses available, in both instances, from local police stations.

In ENGLAND and WALES, applications for Occasional Permission are heard at the Transfer Sessions of the Magistrates' Court in question, usually once a month. Application forms, together with the fee (at present £4), must be received by the Clerks to the Justices at least *one month* before the function and at least *two weeks* before the Transfer Sessions.

(In SCOTLAND, notice has to be given to the Chief Constable of the area, not less than twenty-four hours before the event. The fee for Occasional Permission is currently under review.)

No more than four Occasional Permissions will be granted to any one organisation during twelve consecutive calendar months. Application must be made by a member of the voluntary organisation requiring the Occasional Permission, who must be resident in the area in which the function is to be held.

Information will also be required regarding the precise nature of the voluntary organisation and the type of function at which the bar is to be held, plus the type of intoxicating liquor which is to be sold – i.e. whether Occasional Permission is needed for a beer tent, wine bar, wines and spirits, etc. The applicant may have to appear at the Transfer Sessions, at least on the first occasion.

See also, leaflet TP27 'The Provision of Alcohol on Charity Premises' issued free-of-charge by The Charity Commissioners for England and Wales (available by post to all areas, ref. page 121) and 'Bars, Charities and the Law' published by the National Federation of Community Organisations, 10 Bayley Street, London, WC1B 3HB – telephone: 01-636 1295/6 (price at time of going to press – £9, postage extra, £4 to N.F.C.O. members).

7. SQUARE DANCES
Send a stamped, addressed envelope to:

Mr Jim Ive, President
British Association of American Square Dance Clubs
64 Marlborough Drive
RUISLIP Middlesex

asking for the names of any square dance callers operating in your area and what their fees are likely to be.

8. DARTS TOURNAMENTS
The British Darts Organisation say that the easiest and quickest way to obtain advice is to contact players and organisers in local leagues affiliated to pubs and social clubs.

Although willing to assist fund-raising groups, the organisation's work in promoting professional competitions is such that other enquiries take a little while before they can be answered.

However, if a group is experiencing particular difficulty or needs specific advice on the number of players in a tournament, entry fee to charge competitors, etc. then The British Darts Organisation may be

contacted by telephone: 01-883 5544/5 or write to:
    The British Darts Organisation
    2 Pages Lane Muswell Hill
    LONDON N10 1PS

9. FURTHER INFORMATION ON INCOME TAX, CORPORATION TAX AND
CAPITAL GAINS TAX may be obtained from:
    Inland Revenue (Claims Branch)
    St John's House Merton Road BOOTLE
    Merseyside L69 6BB

For INFORMATION ON INHERITANCE TAX – write to:
    Inland Revenue (Inheritance Tax Enquiries)
    Minford House Rockley Road
    LONDON W14 0DF

10. VALUE ADDED TAX
For a copy of the V.A.T. leaflet 701/1/84 – 'Charities', contact:
    H.M. Customs and Excise
    King's Beam House 39/41 Mark Lane
    LONDON EC3R 7HE

11. 'CHARITIES GUIDE TO V.A.T.' is published by:
    The National Council for Voluntary Organisations
    26 Bedford Square LONDON WC1B 3HU

12. NOTES FOR GUIDANCE ON THE LOTTERIES AND AMUSEMENTS ACT
1976, is published by:
    The Gaming Board for Great Britain
    Africa House 64-78 Kingsway
    LONDON WC2B 6BD

'LOTTERIES AND GAMING. VOLUNTARY ORGANISATIONS AND THE LAW'
is published by The National Council for Voluntary Organisations (see
above).

13. TO APPLY FOR THE REGISTRATION OF A CHARITY IN SCOTLAND write
to:
    H.M. Inspector of Taxes Claims Branch
    Trinity Park House South Trinity Road
    EDINBURGH EH5 3SD
(For Northern Ireland and Eire, please refer to page 122.)

14. FOR A LIST OF SOLICITORS EXPERIENCED IN CHARITY LAW apply to:
    The Law Society
    113 Chancery Lane LONDON WC2A 1PL
Approximate fee for complete service, in the region of £400 for a solicitor
to plan, draw up and submit a constitution for the registration of a charity.

Index

ELLIOT RIGHT WAY BOOKS,
KINGSWOOD, SURREY, U.K.